MY MS JOURNEY
"SPRITUALLY, MENTALLY, EMOTIONALLY AND PHYSICALLY"

MULTIPLE SCLEROSIS
I AM A MS WARRIOR

FIGHTING MS

22 DAYS OF PRAYER, SCRIPTURE, JOURNALING, AND DAILY INSPIRATION!

HOPE
"HELPING OTHER PEOPLE EXCEL"

BY DR. THERESA BASKIN
A NEW LIFE OF COMMUNION WITH GOD IS ABOUT TO OPEN AS YOU READ THIS INCREDILBLE BOOK!

Copyright @ 2022 by Dr. Theresa Baskin

Copyright, Legal Notice and Disclaimer:

When you start reading, you might want to begin by making sure that you have enough time and space to complete this journey. This book is an insightful analysis of the emotions experienced by a person coping with the effects of a long-term health condition. This book is an honest account of my battle with multiple sclerosis (MS), written from the bottom of my heart to inspire and empower other people who are battling a chronic illness. This is a book full with wisdom and insight that can serve as a daily source of motivation for you. Please understand that I am aware that not everybody reacts to life with multiple sclerosis in the same manner. Despite the fact that I can attest from personal experience that it is not easy, I have chosen to proceed along this journey despite the fact that I will face challenges along the way. I sincerely hope that something you read or even take the time to write may prove to be beneficial to you in some way.

Unless otherwise noted, all of the scriptural quotations and references have been taken from various versions of the Holy Bible. These versions include the King James Version, the New King James Version, the New International Version, the Easy English Bible, The Message Bible, the English Standard Version, the Amplified Bible, and the Holy Bible: Easy-to-Read Version. The English Revised Version, the International Standard Version, the New Living Translation, the Good New Translation (US Version), and the New American Standard Bible are all examples of other translations. It is essential to take note of the fact that a list of extra references may be found in the back of the book.

SURVIVING MULTIPLE SCLEROSIS

TABLE OF CONTENTS

ACKNOWLEDGEMENTS

I would like to take this opportunity to express my gratitude to everyone who has shown support and encouragement to me along the course of this journey and who has been there for me. Before everything else, I would like to thank My Lord and Savior Jesus Christ. I am fully aware that this has not been an easy journey for me, but I would like to take this time to thank you, **my family, my coworkers, and my friends, as well as my doctors, therapists, and physical therapists, and most of all Gaylord Specialty Healthcare Center** *for being by my side throughout it all. Throughout the course of my journey, each and every one of you has been a source of inspiration and encouragement for me. I am grateful. Because of the many ways in which you've assisted me, may the Lord continue to shower his blessings upon you. Many people were uninformed of my struggle with MS while I was going through it; yet I want you to know that I hold a special place in my heart for you, and for that, I am grateful.*

A man's gift maketh room for him, and bringeth him before great men.

Proverbs 18:16 KJV

A very special thank you goes out to Ms. Alyssa Taglia, "Wednesdays Warrior" on News Channel 8, for providing me with such an incredible life changing experience.

THERESA BASKIN
WEDNESDAY'S WARRIOR

6:45
71°
WTNH.COM

Social worker continues to inspire despite MS diagnosis

If you would like to watch my "Wednesday Warrior" Interview, please use the link that is provided below:

https://www.wtnh.com/on-air/wednesdayswarrior/social-worker-continues-to-inspire-despite-ms-diagnos

INTRODUCTION:

You have accepted the task of confronting the present by making the decision to read this book, and you are actively participating in the process of positively shaping your future by doing so. Come on, let's get through this journey together and see it through to the end! Please keep in mind that despite the fact that you can be suffering from a variety of illnesses, those illnesses do not control you. After a certain amount of time has passed and you have been forced to endure a number of difficulties, you will finally be able to experience the greatness that was promised to you. It's likely that you, like me, don't fully understand it right now, but God does have a plan for each of our lives. He's got us all figured out. Your life will be

profoundly impacted if you make the effort to join me on my journey through Multiple Sclerosis. I'm going to start at the beginning of my journey and go all the way through my day-to-day struggles, accomplishments, and setbacks. You will spend the next 22 days reading through my multiple sclerosis journey, which will include devotional readings, prayers, thoughts of motivation, and journaling about your own observations and experiences. I believe that every obstacle you face is preparing you for the next step in your journey. My journey will serve as a source of motivation, encouragement, and strength for you to get through the challenges you face on your own journey.

Behold, how good and how pleasant it is for brethren to dwell together in unity!

Psalm 133:1 KJV

MY JOURNEY WITH
MULTIPLE SCLEROSIS

"For I know the plans I have for you," says the LORD. "They are plans for good and not for disaster, to give you a future and a hope."

Jeremiah 29:11 NIV

MY MS JOURNEY

Many are the afflictions of the righteous, But the Lord delivers him out of them all.

Psalm 34:19 NKJV

The 28th of September 2019 was a day that forever altered the course of my life. I have been given a diagnosis of multiple sclerosis. My battle with multiple sclerosis has been a difficult one. It is frightening, in fact it is quite scary. I wake up every morning giving thanks to God because despite the constant pain, numbness, weakness, and fatigue, I was able to make it through the night. Hearing that I struggle from a condition that can severely limit my life was undoubtedly the most difficult thing for me. I am a young woman that is vivacious, joyful, and full of energy. Since I was first diagnosed with a debilitating disease for which there is no cure, I have come a long way. Multiple sclerosis (MS) is a disease that can affect any part of the central nervous system, including the brain, the optic nerve, and the spinal cord. The fact that the body's immune system assaults its own nerves makes MS a challenging disease. Every day, there are a number of challenges that must be addressed. It is hard to live in a world where every moment is different because of how unique it is. The fight against multiple sclerosis (MS) might put you in a position where you question whether or not you will ever be able to get back up again especially with all you deal with from the unknown, the pain, weakness, numbness, fatigue and just to name a few. I will never stop putting my faith in God and his promises that I shall get better. I'm here to tell you that you have the ability to get yourself back up again. Do not let the things that you are unable to do distract you from the things that you are capable of doing. The fact that multiple sclerosis is so little understood by others and those close to you is a frustrating reality. The fact that no one else can even begin to understand what is going on for me and inside of me makes living with pain an extremely challenging experience.

The Bible tells me this in 2 Corinthians 4:17-18: For our light affliction, which is but for a moment, worketh for us a far more exceeding and eternal weight of glory; while we look not at the things which are seen, but at the things which are not seen: for the things which are seen are temporal; but the things which are not seen are eternal. Living through it is the only way to have a true comprehension of our life cycle, which can only be grasped in its totality when examined from a retrospective point of view. My personal experience has taught me that not all storms are sent your way with the purpose of making your life more challenging; rather, some of them are sent to help clear the way for you. I can say without a shadow of a doubt that each and every day of my life has provided me with an incredible and interesting experience of some kind or another. Since the moment of my birth to this very day, I can say that nobody or anything else except God has been in charge of my life. I believe that in this life we are destined to go through certain circumstances, and that God allows things to happen to us so that our faith can grow as a result of those experiences. In addition, I am of the opinion that in order to have a testimony that God will get you out of that situation, you sometimes need to go through something in order to have the experience that would allow you to testify to that fact. I am convinced that the grace of God is more than enough for you, and that his power is displayed most clearly in your weaknesses.

When I think back to when I was a child, I can remember a lot of things that I don't think I fully comprehended until much later in my life. This is something that comes to me when I think about the past. Being born in a prison, graduating with my PhD degrees, being diagnosed with multiple sclerosis, being forced to retire disabled, being forced to downsize from your home due to my MS, falling down the stairs on a number of occasions, you don't get the same income, and writing a book about my journey with MS while still not knowing the outcome of what is considered to be an illness that causes blindness, paralysis with the chance of landing you in a wheel chair or bedridden, cognitive and memory issues, and slurred speech are all the things I worry about. When you talk with other people and they keep encouraging you to have faith and believe God for your healing and so many other words, there were days and moments when I wanted to give up and throw in the towel. I felt alone, frustrated, and disappointed. In spite of this, I have learned *through personal experience that it is essential for one's mental health to be able to express oneself through writing at some point during the process of healing. Despite having multiple sclerosis, I've come to realize that my calling in life is to propel other people toward their goals by motivating, encouraging, and inspiring them, and then pushing them (until something happens) despite all of this! Giving anything and everything back has been the driving force behind everything I've done in my life, right from the start. What has already taken place to me is beyond my control, but I am in charge of what takes place in the **HERE** and **NOW**! Because there is no other option, I have no choice but to make the most of this moment in my life.*

*When I was reading the Bible, I came across a **Love Story** that Christ wrote for us to use as a guide while we are still here on earth. He wrote it so that we can learn from it and apply its lessons to our own relationships. It was **Love** that brought me freedom, that keeps me alive, that guides me, and that watches over me! I have a very solid understanding of **Love**, the power that it possesses, and the reality that if we do not have **Love**, we are nothing as a result of the experiences that we have had in our lifetimes. Because of the various experiences that I've had, I've been able to get this kind of knowledge. Because of the **Love** that God has for me, you were prepared to give up everything for me, including your life on the cross. This demonstrates how much you care about me. Although not all storms are destined to end your life, some of them have the*

14

*potential to make room for something in your life that will bring you greater fulfillment. Instead of concentrating on the journey as a whole, give the step that is immediately in front of you your undivided attention. I wanted to share this **Love** story that Christ wrote for us to read and use as a guide to how we should spend our lives while we are here on earth. He intended for us to read it and use it as a way to learn more about how we should **Love** one another. **Love** is what set me free, what keeps me alive, what leads me, and what maintains a watchful eye over me! **Love** is the approach that I'm going about writing my MS journey. Come on, let's go on this journey together, and let's **Live, Live, Live (LIVE IN VICTORY EVERY DAY)!***

The Best Story of Love That Has Ever Been Given:

Though I speak with the tongues of men and of angels, but have not love, I have become sounding brass or a clanging cymbal. And though I have the gift of prophecy, and understand all mysteries and all knowledge, and though I have all faith, so that I could remove mountains, but have not love, I am nothing. And though I bestow all my goods to feed the poor, and though I give my body to be burned, but have not love, it profits me nothing.

Love suffers long and is kind; love does not envy; love does not parade itself, is not puffed up; does not behave rudely, does not seek its own, is not provoked, thinks no evil; does not rejoice in iniquity, but rejoices in the truth; bears all things, believes all things, hopes all things, endures all things.

Love never fails. But whether there are prophecies, they will fail; whether there are tongues, they will cease; whether there is knowledge, it will vanish away. For we know in part, and we prophesy in part. But when that which is perfect has come, then that which is in part will be done away.

When I was a child, I spoke as a child, I understood as a child, I thought as a child; but when I became a man, I put away childish things. For now, we see in a mirror, dimly, but then face to face. Now I know in part, but then I shall know just as I also am known And now abide faith, hope, love, these three; but the greatest of these is love.

1 Corinthians Chapter 13 verses 1-13KJV

Before We Begin This Journey Let Us Pray:

Dear Heavenly Father, I would like to make a peculiar request of you at this time. Because of the love that you have, I was able to come into being. Every time I take a breath, every time I wake up in the morning, and every single second of every hour, I am under your command. I come to you in utter submission, pleading with you, Father, to lay your hands on me and bestow some of your wisdom. Because the fact that you created me from nothing suggests that you have the capacity to create me once more. I ask you to let the healing power of your spirit to flow into me. Take away from within me anything that does not belong in this situation. Fix the things that need to be fixed. Remove all of the pain and treat any sickness that you identify. Please Lord let the warmth of your healing love to flow through my body and transform any diseased parts into new ones, so that my body can carry out the functions that you intended for it to carry out when you created it. Thank you Lord for hearing my prayer and answering it. And Father, restore me to total health, not just in my mind but also in my body, so that I may continue to serve

18

you until the very end of my life. In the name of Jesus Christ, the Lord of all, I make this petition to you. Amen

MY JOURNEY WITH MULTIPLE SCLEROSIS

It is possible that you will be forced off your journey or distracted along the way, but you should always get back up and try again; you should never settle for less than what you are capable of doing.

LET'S BEGIN

DAY ONE:

MY MS JOURNEY OF BEING DIAGNOSED WITH MS MULTIPLE SCLEROSIS

*My life totally changed on September 28, 2019, when I was diagnosed with MS. Multiple Sclerosis is a chronic debilitating disease that attacks the central nervous system, including the brain, optic nerves, and spinal cord. The body's immune system attacks its own nerves. There's no CURE, and illness progression varies widely. During the course of my research, I discovered that it is believed that there are 2.5 million people around the world who are living with MS. It is estimated that each week in the United States, 200 new cases of the disease are diagnosed. MS is not easy. **I'M SCREAMING IT OUT LOUD...IT IS NOT EASY**!!! Everyday there are many hurdles to jump. Every moment is different and becomes beyond exhausting. MS is a battle that can knock you down so low, until you don't know if you will or can ever get back-up, **BUT GOD!** I had to believe God and his Word that I will **BOUNCE** back again! Despite my pain, the diagnosis, anger, fear, frustration, disappointment, and doubt, as well as everything else that comes with the possibility that one day I could end up blind, bedridden, or using a wheelchair.*

I was having a really terrible day, and I recall sitting in my room crying and having a breakdown at one point. I was furious with God and kept asking him, "Why me? Why me? What did I do to deserve this?" I was extremely upset, and I needed to know the reason WHY!!! I heard a still small voice, that said your "GIFT" will open numerous doors and help you meet important individuals. I literally stopped crying and asked God, "What did you just say?" as I pondered what he had just said. He stated that your GIFT will clear the way for you and bring an overwhelming number of people to you. I was sitting there thinking about it while reflecting on my life up to that point and said to myself, "WAIT, I was born with this condition, and to say the least, it has been a GIFT!" It is not simply about the multiple sclerosis; rather, it is about the purpose that has been assigned to each of us here on earth. Others whom I've met who have MS undoubtedly thought to themselves, "How can I say that given what you go through with MS?" I can only say that because God has guided and directed me while on this journey.

I REALIZE THAT WE ARE NOT ALONE!!!

*The journey through life is not without its bumps. In life, you're going to run into some obstacles; that's just the way things are. Life is not without its challenges, and when they arise, we must activate our faith, our patience, and the power of the word to overcome them. Then, we must learn to **"Live"** in such a way that we are victorious every day, and we must also learn to **"Live"** in such a way that we are free every day. I'm here to tell you that you can get back up **AGAIN** and **AGAIN** and **AGAIN**!*

You might have been diagnosed with MS, but MS doesn't have YOU!

MS JOURNEY SCRIPTURE

Fear not, for I am with you; Be not dismayed, for I am your God. I will strengthen you, Yes, I will help you, I will uphold you with My righteous right hand.

Isaiah 41:10 NKJV

MY MS JOURNEY PRAYER

Dear Father, I thank you for another opportunity to come before you and say thank you. Thank you for another day to live move and have my being. Father, please give me the strength to endure this situation, and to find the blessings and healing that is contains. Please give me the endurance to continue to press forward. Father you said "is there any sick among you? Let him call for the elders of the church, and let them pray over him, anointing him with oil in the name of the Lord." Father, please guide my thoughts, words, and actions so that I walk your path of peace, love, and healing in Jesus Name.

MY MS JOURNEY MOTIVATIONAL THOUGHT OF THE DAY

*Don't Judge me and don't think I'm stupid or mentally disabled. It's not all in my head and I'm not making this up. Having a chronic illness is the **hardest thing** to come to terms with but I **FIGHT & I'M STRONG**! I'm still going to live my life, just like*

you. Don't feel sorry for me. Put yourself in my shoes understand
__ME__. Be there for me and __PLEASE SUPPORT ME!__

DATE: _____

Considering your diagnosis, how have you been handling it?
How do you handle the challenges you're facing right now?

_____

_____

_____

_____

_____

_____

_____

_____

_____

_____

_____

_____

_____

_____

_____

_____

_____

_____

_____

_____

_____

SURVIVING MULTIPLE SCLEROSIS

DAY TWO:

MY MS JOURNEY OF DENIAL

Denial, Denial, Denial *when my doctor told me on 9/28/19, I have Multiple Sclerosis (MS), I literally become numb. The thoughts that went through my mind, only one could imagine. The very first thought without hesitation was, I'm going to die. At that time after all I went through, MRI's, bloodwork, spinal tap, chronic pain, lightheaded, dizziness and so much more. But God! I can't tell you I went to God, or I decreed healing but what I can say is don't really on man for anything. Instead of me turning to God, I started telling people I was diagnosed with MS. Listen, people can be unintentionally insensitive. I realized my other body didn't look like anything was wrong with me. I kept myself together from my head to my toe despite the chronic pain and all the other issues that come with having MS. I realized that people keep telling me don't receive it you don't have MS. I know what the doctor told you, but you don't have MS. At this time, I am angry at people who are connected to me both family and friends because they didn't hear me or understand what I was going through. But God! People were looking at Theresa the woman who loves God, preacher, teacher, mentor, motivational speaker, musician and so much more. I had to come to a place and understand my diagnosis and go to God and not look for people to understand what I didn't. I went to God for myself, and God said to me the doctor told you have MS, but MS*

doesn't have you and your gift will make room for you. At this point,
I'm like foreal God my Gift. There is no cure for multiple sclerosis,
and it progressively gets worst overtime. I'm telling you whatever
the diagnosis you must still believe God. This is a very scary journey
But God! *The Lord said he will never leave me alone and I believe*
God!!!

Denial-the action of declaring something to be untrue!

MY MS JOURNEY SCRIPTURE FOR DENIAL

The righteous cry, and the LORD heareth, and delivereth them
out of all their troubles. The LORD is nigh unto them that are of
a broken heart; and saveth such as be of a contrite spirit. Many
are the afflictions of the righteous: but the LORD delivereth him
out of them all.

Psalm 34:19 KJV

MY MS JOURNEY PRAYER

Heavenly Father, you are the God of all hope and I look to you in
my time of need. Father God, I have searched all over, and I
couldn't find nobody but you. Thank you for in you I know that all
things are possible. Father, please hold my heart within Yours, and
renew my mind, body, and soul. Thank you, Father, for your Grace
and Mercy. Father, you have given me life and you have also given
me the gift of unlimited joy. Thank You in Jesus Name

MY MS JOURNEY MOTIVATIONAL THOUGHT OF THE DAY

*Have **Faith in Yourself** and the ability you possess to direct the course of your own life daily. Have **Faith in the Power** that is deep inside you, and your faith will assist in pointing you in the right direction. Have **Faith in the Future** and all that it has to offer. Your perseverance will be rewarded if you keep a hopeful heart. Because everything will fall into place if you have **Faith and Trust** that **YOU** are capable of **Anything and Everything**!*

DATE: _____

**When trauma isn't dealt with, people tend to deny its existence.
When faced with the fear of reality, how do you usually react?**

_____

_____

_____

_____

_____

_____

_____

_____

_____

_____

_____

_____

_____

_____

_____

_____

_____

_____

_____

_____

SURVIVING MULTIPLE SCLEROSIS

DAY THREE:

MY MS JOURNEY OF WHY ME?

Why Me, Why Me, Why Me? On a daily basis, I sit in my home alone and ask myself and God.....Why Me, Why Me, Why Me! I heard a still small voice say to me, "Why not you?" I sat there contemplating the logic of that; why not me! I had a good life; I was working and giving back to others who may have been struggling or dealing with the ills of society; I was working diligently toward obtaining my PhD; I was mentoring others; I was preaching, teaching, and leading community trainings; and I was doing all of these things and more. I came to the realization that sometimes life may give us curve balls that can leave us feeling down, angry, unsure, and upset.

*I had to accept the fact that everyone in life has a story to tell. Each of us has our own unique life path. It's critical, I've learned, to understand who you are and why you're here. I recognize that whatever physical, spiritual, or mental obstacles I face, there is a reason for them. I constantly remind people not to make comparisons between their lives and those of others; the sun and the moon are totally opposite. They shine when the circumstances call for it, regardless of the difficulties you face in life.... Refrain from loosening your grip on God's hand! Continue forward; **DO NOT LOOK BACK**!!! What you need is before you not behind you! Every day, Live, Live, Live (LIVE IN VICTORY EVERY DAY!)*

MY MS JOURNEY SCRIPTURES FOR WHY ME

And we know that all things work together for good to them that love God, to them who are the called according to his purpose.

Romans 8:28 KJV

"I knew you before I formed you in your mother's womb. Before you were born, I set you apart and appointed you as my prophet to the nations."

Jeremiah 1:5 KJV

MY MS JOURNEY PRAYER

God, please grant me peace and tranquility, I need to make it through this journey. To accept the things that I am powerless to change; Courage to change what I am capable of changing; and wisdom to discern the difference. Taking each day as it comes; Taking each moment in stride; Accepting obstacles in life as a necessary step toward peace; Taking this sinful world as it is, rather than as I would have it; Trusting that God will make all things right if I submit to His Will; that I may be reasonably happy in this life and eternally happy with Him in the next.

In Jesus Name Amen

MY MS JOURNEY MOTIVATIONAL THOUGHT OF THE DAY

*You are not bound by obstacles. **Life is Short**.*
*If you **RUN** into a roadblock, do not turn around and quit.*
Determine a way to scale it, navigate around it, or pass through it!

DATE: _____

How do you deal with the perpetual "Why Me?" sensation if it seems like the whole world is conspiring against you?

_____

_____

_____

_____

_____

_____

_____

_____

_____

_____

_____

_____

_____

_____

_____

_____

_____

_____

_____

_____

SURVIVING MULTIPLE SCLEROSIS

DAY FOUR:

MY MS JOURNEY OF ANGER

Anger, Anger, Anger that's an **Understatement!** *It is believed that the demyelination that can occur in certain areas of the brain as a result of multiple sclerosis can lead to the development of the emotional complication of anger. Don't let anger change who you are in a bad way! Having a chronic illness such as multiple sclerosis is accompanied by a variety of feelings. Sadness, fear, guilt, despair, shame, and anxiety are among the numerous negative emotions. It is an exhaustive list containing both positive and negative experiences. In cases such as mine, my damaged brain seems to trigger a flood of these emotions almost at random, resulting in mood swings and situations that tend to conceal how I truly feel. I've heard numerous times that this can manifest externally as one of the most frightening emotions,* **ANGER!** *Despite having valid reasons to be angry, I am rarely as angry as I may appear at times.*

Despite the fact that I keep a constant smile on my face and make jokes most of the time. Because of what I am going through, I am feeling a great deal of **ANGER!** *However, I have come to the conclusion that it is perfectly acceptable to not be okay. Therefore, when you have a disease that cannot be cured, there are times when you have very good reasons to feel* **ANGRY!** *Accepting the changes in one's life is more than sufficient to provoke* **ANGER** *in a person. You grow up believing that your life will be a certain way, you work* *hard to make that happen, everything is going well, and then suddenly, out of the blue, you become ill. It's as if you're in the lead of a race for which you've trained your entire life, and then a shark appears out of nowhere and grabs you. Except that it does not kill you; instead, it deforms you and dashes your hopes. I'm sure that many chronically ill individuals are constantly angry about their circumstances. How could you possibly resist? Particularly if you are a fighter who has not given up. I freely admit that I become extremely upset by my predicament.*

Often, however, this anger propels me to continue fighting, to continue battling, and to demonstrate to the disease, the world, and myself that the shark that mauled me will not prevent me from finishing the race. People who were angry about something that happened to them and channeled that anger produced some of the greatest performances in history. So yes, I am furious with my illness, and I am constantly fighting it! However, this anger can emerge when I least expect it. I may be in a fighting mindset and be forced to switch gears abruptly. Sadly, I am aware that this shift is not always successful, and I may appear angry at someone when I am actually angry at my disease.

MY MS JOURNEY SCRIPTURE

"In your anger do not sin" Do not let the sun go down while you are still angry, and do not give the devil a foothold. Anyone who has been stealing must steal no longer, but must work, doing something useful with their own hands, that they may have something to share with those in need.

Ephesians 4:26-31 KJV
MY MS JOURNEY PRAYER

Your peace, Eternal God, surpasses my understanding. When my anger flares, please use your kind words to soothe my mind and heart. I ask you, Father, to please whisper words of comfort to me that will relieve both my mind and my heart whenever I feel my anger beginning to rise. Fill my entire life with your unconditional peace. May your peace shape my personality rather than my frustration. With the presence of your Holy Spirit in my life, I can overcome my anger. May I reflect your character by being slow to anger and full of unwavering love. Consider me and let your face shine upon me. Through our Lord Jesus Christ, Amen.

MY MS JOURNEY MOTIVATIONAL THOUGHT OF THE DAY

*Rest in me. I am prepared to work in your life, so keep your mind on the task at hand, and I will turn every negative situation in your life around. Don't be **ANGRY**; instead, **FIGHT, FIGHT, FIGHT!!!***

DATE: _____

How can I learn to let out my anger in a healthy way that doesn't make me feel like a victim?

_____

_____

_____

_____

_____

_____

_____

_____

_____

_____

_____

_____

_____

_____

_____

_____

_____

_____

DAY FIVE:

MY MS JOURNEY OF FEAR

Fear, Fear, Fear MS is often accompanied by fear. Fear is likely to have been a very significant factor in your life, especially if multiple sclerosis (MS) has been diagnosed with you or someone you care about. The experience starts out with strange symptoms, which are followed by the fear of not understanding why one is having those symptoms. Fear can become overpowering and even incapacitating. Facing one's fears head on is something that many people living with multiple sclerosis (MS) may face at various moments during the course of their journey. Fear is pervasive and has multiple layers, but if I gave into it constantly, I would never get out of bed, challenge myself, or accomplish anything.

*On this path, many people living with multiple sclerosis (MS) are confronted with alarming symptoms as well as recurring, relapsing, and progressively more severe multiple sclerosis. I can tell with certainty that fear is a crippling emotion that prevents one from moving forward and keeps one stuck in a place of isolation. The more I studied about multiple sclerosis by perusing reliable websites, connecting with people on social media, and going to my multiple sclerosis support group on a monthly basis, the less I worried about the future. You cannot predict your prognosis because no two MS patients are identical. **MS is not a death*** *__sentence__; instead, we must learn to live with it and manage it as best we can!*

Since the day I was first diagnosed with multiple sclerosis until now, I've been plagued by a strong urge to avoid making other people's lives more difficult as a result of my condition, which has been a constant source of frustration for me. It doesn't matter if I'm in need of assistance with the activities of daily living, in chronic pain or if I'm just talking about my condition; I always have this nagging worry in my mind that I might be making someone else's life more difficult, making them feel uncomfortable, or negatively interfering with their routines in some way. This worry is rooted in my personal history, my character, independence, and the desire to be recognized for qualities other than my sickness; unfortunately, it has a negative impact on my wellbeing. Throughout this entire ordeal with multiple sclerosis, I have consistently put my faith in God's word. In Isaiah 41:10, the Bible addresses the topic of fear; __Do not be afraid__ for I am with you; do not be dismayed for I am your God; I will strengthen you; I will help you; I will uphold you with my righteous right hand.

MY MS JOURNEY SCRIPTURE FOR FEAR
For God has not given us a spirit of fear, but of power and of love and of a sound mind.

2 Timothy 1:7 NKJV

MY MS JOURNEY PRAYER

Dear Lord, You are aware that we live in a chaotic world. You are also aware of my daily struggles. When life becomes overwhelming, please assist me in coming to you. Calm my mind and heart, and fill me with your peace, comfort, and wisdom. Help me to live without fear. Please help ease the fear and anxiety that plague me. As I navigate this broken world, help me to rest in You and trust in You. In Your name, Jesus, I pray. Amen.

MY MS JOURNEY MOTIVATIONAL THOUGHT OF THE DAY

F.E.A.R

FALSE EVIDENCE APPEARING REAL!!!!

DATE: _____

When I most recently experienced this particular fear, how did I respond to the situation? Will I be able to come up with an alternative response to how I feel about that situation?

_____

_____

_____

_____

_____

_____

_____

_____

_____

_____

_____

_____

_____

_____

_____

_____

_____

_____

_____

_____

SURVIVING MULTIPLE SCLEROSIS

DAY SIX:

MY MS JOURNEY OF STRESS

*MS is unpredictable, which may cause **STRESS!** The disease can deteriorate and transform without warning. MS is physically debilitating. The effort required to live with and manage the disease is taxing and may lead to emotional strain. Some of the practical repercussions of multiple sclerosis, such as missing work or falling behind on essential tasks, can also contribute to feelings of being overwhelmed. Multiple sclerosis is not caused by stress, according to the available evidence. However, stress can make managing MS symptoms more difficult. In addition, stress has triggered and exacerbated my MS symptoms causing a relapse. Stress cannot be considered a cause of multiple sclerosis, but it can be a significant factor in relapses and hospital stays. There are numerous studies indicating that stressful life events are associated with a significant increase in the risk of MS exacerbation in the weeks or months following the onset of the stressor among MS patients. A significant source of stress is the absence of visible symptoms and the presence of significant concerns about the cost of treatment and the need for ongoing adjustments to combat the progression of a disease.*

I had never given any thought to the possibility of being affected by a disease that could change the course of my life, so when I found out I had one, I did not really know how to react. Every time I am reminded of my condition, I am still taken aback by the severity of it. My journey with MS has taught me to employ effective stress management techniques. Meditation has been shown to influence parts of the brain that can help you respond to stress more efficiently, according to scientific studies. Exercise not only reduces stress by releasing endorphins, but it also enhances your entire sense of well-being, particularly if you enjoy the physical exercise while chatting with others. Diet can also help with chronic stress, which generates cortisol, which increases the desire for calorie-dense, sweet, fatty, processed meals, according to studies. A poor diet can cause gut inflammation, which can result in an MS recurrence. A good night's sleep is essential for reducing stress since it will help you better manage any stress that comes your way. A minimum of seven to eight hours of sleep is required each night.

Understanding Multiple Sclerosis and what you must do to maintain a healthy, stress-free lifestyle is essential. Yes, believe me, although it may be challenging, it is achievable!!!

MY MS JOURNEY SCRIPTURE

Be careful for nothing; but in everything by prayer and supplication with thanksgiving let your requests be made known unto God.

Philippians 4:6 KJV

Peace I leave with you, my peace I give unto you: not as the world giveth, give I unto you.

John 14:27 KJV

MY MS JOURNEY PRAYER

Lord, thank you for desiring for us to surrender our worries to you. Thank you for the fact that there is nowhere I can go where you are not present. Thank you for having control over my life, despite the fact that I feel as though everything is crumbling around me.

Lord, I acknowledge that I have allowed stress to control my life instead of You. I have allowed stress to dictate my disposition, attitudes, and actions. I repent of this, Lord! Please, Father, help me to understand the stressful situations in my life and to surrender them to You. Help me to not let stress win. Assist me in actively reflecting on Your goodness to me.

I look forward to an eternity with you, Lord, in which there will be NO stress! Assist me in remembering all the times You have rescued me from stressful situations and give me hope for a future in which You will eliminate all stress forever.

Please grant me the grace to face the challenges of this day with faith in the reality of Your goodness and power. Many thanks, Lord. In Jesus' Name, Amen.

MY MS JOURNEY MOTIVATIONAL THOUGHT OF THE DAY

*God, please give me the sense of **Peace** to accept the circumstances that I cannot alter.*

*The **Bravery** to change what **I** can and the sagacity to distinguish between what **I** can and cannot **Change!***

43

DATE: _____

When was the last time you felt overwhelmed by stress? How do you manage the stress that you experience in your daily life?

_____

_____

_____

_____

_____

_____

_____

_____

_____

_____

_____

_____

_____

_____

_____

_____

_____

_____

_____

_____

SURVIVING MULTIPLE SCLEROSIS

DAY SEVEN:

MY MS JOURNEY OF DOUBT

It's difficult to overcome self-doubt and find ways to increase self-confidence when you're dealing with a chronic illness. This is especially true if the self-doubt gremlin is perched on your shoulder, whispering negative ideas into your ear. You understand what I'm talking about. Lack of knowledge about multiple sclerosis makes it easier for skepticism to arise, especially in emotionally charged situations. When your body regularly betrays you and your life is defined by your day-to-day health, it's difficult to maintain a good sense of self.

It might be much more complicated to communicate your concerns to those who have never lived through what you are going through if they have never had multiple sclerosis. Managing the uncertainty that comes with having multiple sclerosis can be very difficult. As a consequence of this, it is not unusual for people who do not have a comprehensive understanding of the nature of your disease to express doubt toward those unpredictable symptoms. When your family and friends are unable to recognize a pattern in your symptoms and are unable to recognize for themselves when you are experiencing them, it is possible for them to form incorrect ideas, doubts, and questions about why you are unable to do something that you were able to easily do the day before. People who are close to you could wonder if you are exaggerating your symptoms or even fake them to get people's sympathy or to get out of doing something you don't want to do. This kind of mistrust and uncertainty from the people you care about the most may obviously cause you a great deal of pain and put a significant strain on your relationship. Because of this, you shouldn't judge a book based solely on its cover.

Please stop being so critical of yourself. Through this journey with multiple sclerosis, I found that the majority of people are their own worst critics and are less forgiving of themselves than they would be of a stranger. We have conversations with ourselves that we would never have with a friend. This weakens our good thoughts about ourselves and might contribute to the destruction of self-esteem. I am very aware that I am not my chronic condition and that it does not define me, yet the truth is that it controls a significant portion of my life. But in spite of everything that is going on, I've come to the realization that having hope means being able to recognize that there is a glimmer of light at the end of the tunnel.

MY MS JOURNEY SCRIPTURE

Trust in the Lord with all thine heart; and lean not unto thine own understanding. In all thy ways acknowledge him, and he shall direct thy paths.

Proverbs 3:5-6 KJV

MY MS JOURNEY PRAYER

Father God, I pray that you would remove my self-doubt. Help me to see me like you see me. Help me discover my purpose in the life you've given me. I am aware that you value, love, and appreciate me. You fashioned me by hand, and that was no accident. Display the gifts you've given me. Be with me on my journey to discover my true destiny through you. Lord, give me the strength to get past my worries and fears. Build my faith in you. And let me be so strong in you that there is no room for fear or doubt.

In Jesus Name I pray Amen

MY MS JOURNEY MOTIVATIONAL THOUGHT OF THE DAY

__Patience__, __Perseverance__, __Drive__, and, most importantly, __Self-Confidence__ is required for __Success__! You can't deny what you're capable of, so __Believe In Yourself!__

DATE: _____

Do you ever find yourself struggling to believe something that you know to be true? Do you find that you have moments where you struggle with self-doubt? How do you deal with the issues that surface as a direct result of the values that you uphold?

_____

_____

_____

_____

_____

_____

_____

_____

_____

_____

_____

_____

_____

_____

_____

_____

_____

_____

_____

_____

_____

DAY EIGHT:

MY MS JOURNEY OF FATIGUE

FATIGUE IS REAL!!!! *There were many, many days where I was soooooo tired. Almost everyone occasionally struggles with being overworked or overtired at some point. Instances of transient weariness like this typically have a discernible root cause and a potential treatment option. I often wondered why I was so tired. I would go to bed earlier to see if that would help,* __NOTHING HELPED__*! I would pray, sit and cry sometimes because I needed energy to make it through my day! I had a fast pace, job and life which doesn't allow me to be tired all the time.* **Fatigue is a symptom of Multiple Sclerosis!**

__MS Fatigue__ feels like you are weighed down and it's like every moment is difficult or clumsy. It can also feel like extreme jet lag. Fatigue caused by multiple sclerosis (MS) is a severe form of exhaustion, the likes of which can be incapacitating and overpowering. It is possible for it to start unexpectedly and continue on a daily basis, frequently becoming worse as the day progresses. However, fatigue is one of the symptoms that has a significant impact on my day-to-day life and activities.

Aside from that, I have an issue with being overly sensitive to heat, which makes me feel more exhausted when I am in hot situations or when I become overheated. Although I despise the air conditioning, it is of great assistance in preventing me from becoming overheated.

Additionally, it would be beneficial to have a cooling vest. No one will ever understand the effort that I put out each day just to get out of bed and get moving. Remember that my conflict is not an outward one; rather, it is an inner battle that affects both my outer body and the way it functions. It may not appear that way because of the way I look. I'm maintaining day by day and taking one step at a time literally.

Fatigue extreme tiredness resulting from mental or physical exertion or illness: weaken by repeated variations of <u>STRESS!</u>

MY MS JOURNEY SCRIPTURE

He gives power to the faint, and to him who has no might he increases strength. Even youths shall faint and be weary, and young men shall fall exhausted; but they who wait for the Lord shall renew their strength; they shall mount up with wings like eagles; they shall run and not be weary; they shall walk and not faint.

Isaiah 40:29-31 ESV

MY MS JOURNEY PRAYER

I prayed to the Lord asking for him to help me please I am so tired. I need your strength to work from the inside out. Please father give me strength to endure situations in my life and to find the blessings and lessons in which it contains. Father, please give me the endurance to continue ahead. Father, please direct my thoughts, words, and deeds so that I may travel the road of peace and love that you have laid out for me. In Jesus Name

MY MS JOURNEY MOTIVATIONAL THOUGHT OF THE DAY

*Despite the challenges from **DAY** to **DAY**, stay focused and remember! Worry causes **FATIGUE**, not work **FRUSTRATION** and **RESENTMENT**!! Let God be your daily **STRENGTH**!!!*

DATE: _____

In what ways does fatigue impact you?

_____

_____

_____

_____

_____

_____

_____

_____

_____

_____

_____

_____

_____

_____

_____

_____

_____

_____

_____

_____

_____

_____

SURVIVING MULTIPLE SCLEROSIS

DAY NINE:

MY MS JOURNEY OF CHRONIC PAIN

Pain has a distinct voice! **Chronic pain** is an ever-present companion for many people with multiple sclerosis (MS), diminishing their quality of life. However, treating and managing chronic pain in MS patients is difficult. They may be experiencing neuropathic pain, which is caused by damage to the nerves in the central nervous system. Multiple sclerosis is frequently associated with a variety of pain syndromes, including both acute and chronic pain. Chronic pain is an ever-present companion for many people with multiple sclerosis (MS), diminishing their quality of life. However, treating and managing chronic pain in MS patients is difficult. Being in pain frequently is difficult.

Pain transforms you and influences every aspect of your life. Most people with an "invisible" illness, such as MS, are accustomed to putting on a fake smile and carrying on with life while the multitude of symptoms battering their body beneath the surface remain unseen. Sometimes it's impossible to fake a smile, and we may appear angry, disinterested, or in any number of other ways that turn people off. When you cannot see what we are experiencing, it is easy to assume that we are angry or otherwise unpleasant. We're good at putting on phony smiles, but man, it's not easy! It takes a great deal of effort to interact with or even just be around *other people. When my body is in excruciating, burning pain, it is already difficult to hold a conversation. If it's about something that I find even mildly irritating, I may appear angry even if I'm not. This is just one of the many issues associated with living with pain.*

Pain, Pain, Pain *I must literally say that I am constantly in chronic pain. When I'm in pain, I don't want to talk about it or tell others about it because I know that when people look at me, they believe I don't experience any difficulties because I don't complain. Pain is a highly personal experience that can only be felt and not seen by others. It is a common symptom of multiple sclerosis and can limit your ability to engage in enjoyable activities. I have reached a point in my life where I am able to accept and manage my pain. Every single day of my life, I have to go through the struggle of dealing with the discomfort that comes with being in constant pain. But I force myself to get-up, don't look back and **Keep it Moving!** Having MS is extremely difficult and dealing with the pain is an entirely separate issue. I have cried myself to sleep, prayed for myself, and anointed myself. Many medications have been prescribed to me, but they all cause extreme fatigue and mental confusion. I dislike feeling this way very much.*

Show compassion toward individuals who live with considerable pain. It is beyond tiring on all fronts, including the physical, the mental, and the emotional. It's not their fault, and your frustration will only make them feel worse, so try not to take it out on them. Nobody knowingly opts for a life spent in constant pain.

*Please try to have a little more patience. **MS pain takes planning**.*
We have to make preparations for the unforeseen.

Prayer Changes Everything!!!!!

MY MS JOURNEY SCRIPTURE

The righteous cry, and the Lord heareth, and delivereth them out
of all their troubles. The Lord is nigh unto them that are of a
broken heart; and saveth such as be of a contrite spirit.

Psalm 34:17-18 KJV

At least I can take comfort in this: Despite the pain, I have not
denied the words of the Holy One

Job 6:10 NLT

MY MS JOURNEY PRAYER

Father God, we thank you Lord! I am praying for every person
struggling with chronic pain. You're aware of the bodily
discomfort I'm experiencing right now. You already know how
much I can take. I hand over my body to you. I pray that no matter
what occurs, I will be able to put my trust in You! I pray that Your
will be carried out in my life. I beg you, God, to take away the
bodily suffering. Please help me to become better. I also support
people who are in bodily distress. May you anoint their bodies and
heal them. I hope we never take our health for granted. I pray that
whenever You invite us to participate in Your will and it is within
our power to do so, we will. Assist us in appreciating what we are
capable of. May your Holy Spirit instill in us a desire to pray for

others despite our personal suffering. We pray in Jesus' name,

Amen!

MY MS JOURNEY MOTIVATIONAL THOUGHT OF THE DAY

*Some people believe that being strong means never experiencing pain. In truth, the strongest individuals are those who **<u>Feel it</u>**, **<u>Comprehend it</u>**, and **<u>Accept it</u>**!*

DATE: _____

How, in your opinion, does living with chronic pain affect your everyday life and the lives of those closest to you?

_____

_____

_____

_____

_____

_____

_____

_____

_____

_____

_____

_____

_____

_____

_____

_____

_____

_____

_____

SURVIVING MULTIPLE SCLEROSIS

MY MS JOURNEY OF VERTIGO & DIZZINESS

*A condition that affects our body and inhibits us from operating normally as we would is called dizziness. **Dizziness or vertigo** is not a condition that is life threatening, but it might prevent us from engaging in activities of daily living because of the fear that we will fall. In more severe circumstances, dizziness can become a significant condition that can have a negative and sometimes life-threatening influence on our lives. According to the data, more than forty percent of those of us aged 40 and older complain of experiencing blackouts, dizziness, or instability.*

However, there is hope for you in the Word of God, particularly if you have attempted the instructions given to you by your doctor but you are still feeling dizzy. Vertigo is a challenging symptom because it appears and disappears at random times throughout the day. Because of this aspect of the illness, you are really kept in a state of utter fear since the dizziness and vertigo really prohibit you from moving around. Because of my fear and anxiety, I was unable to drive, which severely restricted my mobility given that the room was suddenly turning on its own. Not to mention the feeling of sickness. I would be out in public or even at my place of employment when suddenly, the room would start to spin, and all I could do was try to keep my balance and trust that no one else saw what was happening. I came to the realization that, in more extreme cases, dizziness can become a major problem that might disrupt our lives in a way that is potentially deadly. Because I had no other option, I had no alternative but to pray and ask God for his help with this issue. Believe me when I say that this has been a **Challenging Journey!**

BUT GOD!!!!

MY MS JOURNEY SCRIPTURE

He gives strength to the weary and increases the power of the weak.

Isaiah 40:29 NIV

Lord my God, I called to you for help, and you healed me.

Psalm 30:2 NIV

MY MS JOURNEY PRAYER

Father, I pray thee to have compassion on me and on those around me, and I pray that you will restore our equilibrium and cure us of our vertigo as well as our dizziness. God, you are the all-powerful healer and the one who works miracles and wonders. I continue to have trust that my health will be completely restored. In the name of Jesus, I have faith that you will immediately make me completely whole again, and I ask that you do it right now.

MY MS JOURNEY MOTIVATIONAL THOUGHT OF THE DAY

*The **feeling** of **vertigo** is caused by an **inner battle** between the urge to **Fall** and the sense of **Helplessness! Stay Strong!!!!!***

DATE: _____

Vertigo is defined by a misleading sense that either oneself or one's surroundings are moving or spinning. This feeling can be caused by either the vertigo sufferer themselves or their surroundings. How does having vertigo or dizziness affect the way you go about your day-to-day activities?

_____

_____

_____

_____

_____

_____

_____

_____

_____

_____

_____

_____

_____

_____

_____

_____

_____

_____

SURVIVING MULTIPLE SCLEROSIS

DAY ELEVEN:

MY MS JOURNEY OF WEAKNESS, PARALYSIS, NUMBNESS & TINGLING

Multiple sclerosis (MS) is a condition in which nerve fibers in the central nervous system are damaged. Over time, multiple sclerosis can cause impairments with vision, muscle weakness, loss of balance, and numbness. **Weakness, paralysis, numbness, and tingling** *are all issues I suffer with. For the first time since my diagnosis, I had an* **MS attack** *in June of 2021. It was a disaster. From my chest to my feet, I couldn't feel my body. I couldn't walk and was in excruciating pain. That was the most terrifying experience or place I've ever been. For intense medication treatment, I was admitted to the hospital and stayed for five days. Due to Covid, while in the hospital there were visitation limitations, and there were no guests. It was a frightening event but thank God! With his Grace, Mercy, and Favor, he guided me through this process. It was nothing but the Blood of Jesus. All I can do was to pray and trust in God that I will be able to walk again. I was discharged from the hospital with a walker. I was given nursing care in the comfort of my own home as well as physical therapy for a while. To God alone be the Glory, I am able to walk, and I really don't look like someone who has been through what I have.*

I realized later when I was walking around the track at the local high school for exercise, there were times when the foot of my left foot would go numb and start flopping around. I can still remember those instances. I had no idea what was going on at the time, but whenever it happened, I had to stop what I was doing and loosen the strings on my sneakers in case that was the problem. In addition, for a good portion of my life, I have suffered from swollen, numb, and painful legs. Following my recent MS flare-up, I've noticed that my walking has become more difficult. Because of the unpredictability of the circumstance, all I can do each day is get out of bed, place both feet on the ground, and then thank God for his goodness.

Suppose you could put yourself in my shoes for a moment. What I've come to realize is that when people look at me, they have no idea the struggles that I face on the inside. I'm sorry if I've repeated myself, but this is simply not fair. I have come to the conclusion that I am no longer capable of traveling long distances by vehicles. Simply sitting for extended periods of time brings excruciating pain to my back and legs. Because of the pain and the stiffness, I have no choice but to get up and stretch every so often. My legs do not have the same amount of strength that they once did BUT GOD!!! I'm not going to complain about it; all I'm going to do is share the fact that this is really challenging.

In closing, I feel compelled to express my gratitude to God for the existence of **Gaylord Specialty Healthcare**, which is located in Wallingford, Connecticut. **Aqua and physical therapy** at the outpatient facility of the Gaylord Specialty Healthcare have been *both a life saver and a lifeline for me. I can state without a doubt that I am grateful to God for* **Sue Goldstein, PT** *and* **Ingrid Marschner, PT.** *Both of them have been a blessing to me throughout my MS journey. They have assisted me in a way that is beneficial to both my body and my mind. They have been there for me to listen to, assist, support, and encourage me as I navigate this journey with multiple sclerosis.* **Both of them have been just incredible.** *I would like to express my gratitude to* **Annette Theis, MSPT** *and* **Joy Savulak, Publicist** *for her unwavering support and encouragement as well as for the life-changing opportunities she has made available to me. If you ever find yourself in need of any kind of therapy, I strongly suggest that you check out* **Gaylord Specialty Healthcare in Wallingford, Connecticut.** *I've received physical therapy in the past, but ever since I started coming to Gaylord for treatment, I've been able to fight this debilitating illness with a greater sense of self-assurance.* **"THINK POSSIBLE"!**

MY MS JOURNEY SCRIPTURE

But the Lord said, "My grace is all you need. Only when you are weak can everything be done completely by my power." So, I will gladly boast about my weaknesses. Then Christ's power can stay in me.

2 Corinthians 12:9 ERV

He gives strength to the weary and increases the power of the weak. Even youths grow tired and weary, and young men stumble and fall; but those who hope in the Lord will renew their

strength. They will soar on wings like eagles; they will run and not grow weary; they will walk and not be faint.

Isaiah 40:29-31 KJV

MY MS JOURNEY PRAYER

You, Lord, are aware of the challenges posed by my weakness, paralysis, numbness, and tingling. You, Lord, are aware of the challenges I face. You are aware of my strong desire for healing. I am currently requesting Your healing touch. I have faith in your capacity to heal me. I understand that many things in life are given to test us. Please shine Your light of healing upon me and dispel the darkness and sorrow I am experiencing. Permit Your Love to pour into me. Everything is possible due to your existence. In the name of the Lord Jesus Christ! Amen

MY MS JOURNEY MOTIVATIONAL THOUGHT OF THE DAY

*The **Benefit of Weaknesses** is that they reveal areas in which we need to progress **Physically and Mentally**! It is never too late to continue learning how to become **Stronger**, regardless of age or circumstance.*

S.T.R.O.N.G

STOP

TAKING

GREAT

OPPORTUNITIES

FOR GRANTED

DATE: _____

Tingling and numbness are two of the most frequently experienced physical symptoms of multiple sclerosis (MS). It was impossible to predict when the tingling and numbness would begin. Extreme numbness can make it challenging for a person to use the affected body part, which might disrupt their ability to participate in day-to-day activities.

What are some of the strategies you use to keep up with your everyday activities despite the weakness, tingling, and numbness you're experiencing?

_____

_____

_____

_____

_____

_____

_____

_____

_____

_____

_____

_____

_____

_____

_____

_____

SURVIVING MULTIPLE SCLEROSIS

DAY TWELVE:

MY MS JOURNEY OF DEPRESSION & ANXIETY

From the moment the very first symptoms appear, multiple sclerosis can be a source of substantial anxiety, sadness, anger, and frustration. One of the most distressing elements of multiple sclerosis is the uncertainty and unpredictability that comes along with it. People who have multiple sclerosis really have a significantly higher risk of suffering from anxiety than depression. Both the changes in life circumstances and the severe loss of functions that can be caused by the condition are potential major triggers for anxiousness and frustration in affected individuals. Multiple sclerosis (MS) patients frequently struggle with anxiety, which may be brought on, at least in part, by the inflammation that is characteristic of this condition.

Being diagnosed with multiple sclerosis regrettably comes with a number of side effects, one of which is anxiety, the cause of which I have no idea; yet it is something that I have to face and deal with. There are times when I have to deal with a lot mentally. Anxiety is a separate issue from depression, which is a separate issue entirely. Because I am having a hard time processing the diagnosis and the uncertainty that comes along with it, there are moments when I just sit and cry. Because I have a smile on my face, other people think that everything is well. It in no way represents the truth behind the truth. I am in constant pain, unable to work my career job, unable to perform the things I used to be able to accomplish, sitting or walking for extended periods of time, can't wear my high heel shoes anymore, and just to say the least, my thoughts and mental functioning are altered. I cry so much by myself that eventually I get so emotionally distraught that my gorgeous eye lashes I paid for begin to fall out. There was something more that I kept to myself until now. I have a condition called frontal lobbing alopecia, which causes my hair to fall out in patches. The fact that I have lost so much hair and have bold spots makes people question why I don't wear many different styles. Due to the fact that others are staring at you and thinking what could possibly be wrong with her, I am too embarrassed to go to the hairdresser. As I sit here and type this, I can't help but feel emotional. Man, if only you knew. Because I am confident that God has a purpose for me, I cannot help but keep a smile on my face.

I find it essential to pray every day that I won't find myself in a situation from which there is no escape. It is essential that we grasp the concept that there are certain aspects of life which we have no control over. But if you get out of bed every morning, you'll see that each day is a fresh start, just like I do while going through my MS journey. Because praying and worrying won't change anything but I've realized there's no point in wasting my time with that thought, I might as well just live my life. My hope is that despite the challenges that you might be facing in life, you will be able to live your own life to the fullest extent possible with as much help and *support as you possibly can while you are traveling on this path we call **LIFE!***

MY MS JOURNEY SCRIPTURE

Be anxious for nothing, but in everything by prayer and supplication, with thanksgiving, let your requests be made known to God; and the peace of God, which surpasses all understanding, will guard your hearts and minds through Christ Jesus.

Philippians 4:6-7 NKJV

Casting all your cares all your anxieties, all your worries, and all your concerns, once and for all on Him, for He cares about you with deepest affection, and watches over you very carefully.

1 Peter 5:7 AMP

MY MS JOURNEY PRAYER

Help me, Lord, to develop more faith and hope with each passing day and give me the courage to put my trust in the future that you have planned for me. Raise me up out of my frustration and surround me with your grace as it heals. While we are walking together through each moment of my healing, please teach me to entrust all of my concerns and uncertainties in your hands. Replace the dreary feeling of depression with the joy that can only be found in you. I am grateful for my life, for the hidden blessings you have bestowed upon me, and for the fact that you have never left my side. Amen

MY MS JOURNEY MOTIVATIONAL THOUGHT OF THE DAY

*As if each day were your **Last**, **Live** your **Life** to the **Fullest!!!***

When we spend our entire lives trying to please other people, we put ourselves in a position where we are more likely to experience feelings of tension, anxiety, and depression. How do you manage to get through each day despite all of the stressful events and circumstances that are a regular part of your life?

_____

_____

_____

_____

_____

_____

_____

_____

_____

_____

_____

_____

_____

_____

_____

_____

_____

_____

_____

SURVIVING MULTIPLE SCLEROSIS

DAY THIRTEEN:

MY MS JOURNEY OF COGNITIVE, MEMORY & EMOTIONAL CHALLENGES

People who have problems with their memory as well as their cognitive abilities are the primary audience for this topic. You were having a conversation with someone, and you got off to a fantastic start, but suddenly you can't remember what you were saying because you were distracted by something that threw you off focus. Have you ever been in a situation like that? There are times when we are presented with difficult obstacles that prevent us from achieving our goals. They prevent us from reaching our full potential, preventing us from being more productive, and preventing us from living our lives with purpose and enthusiasm.

They keep us "STUCK."

Because of my struggle with memory and, unfortunately, some cognitive delays, I had to educate myself on a variety of strategies that could assist me. To manage the memory loss, I experience on a day-to-day basis, I make use of a wide variety of memory aids and strategies. I write all of my important appointments and other commitments down on a calendar so that I don't forget them. I remind myself to take my medications, go to my scheduled medical appointments, and finish other tasks by setting reminders on my iPhone or sticking post-it notes around the house. I keep a journal and a notebook next to my bed so that I can record significant ideas and thoughts that I want to remember for the future and use in my journal.

*It is imperative that I continue to pray and have faith in God. Regardless of the challenges I must overcome, I am confident that I will be able to achieve any goal that I set for myself. In answer to your question, yes, we will continue to have hope, we will continue to dream, we will continue to put in a lot of effort, and we will continue to grow. In point of fact, each and every one of us is susceptible to failing at something, falling, and experiencing feelings of hurt, betrayal, and a lack of understanding and compassion from other people. Despite this, we have the ability to pick ourselves up, give it another shot, try again, hope again, dream again, work again, and build once more. We have the potential to achieve success once more. We have the capacity to recover our happiness and sense of fulfillment. Just keep telling yourself that it isn't over and remember to keep your attention on the task at hand. **We can say it together.** I am **Confident** that I will be able to **Finish** this **Task**!*

MY MS JOURNEY SCRIPTURE

Finally, brethren, whatsoever things are true, whatsoever things are honest, whatsoever things are just, whatsoever things are pure, whatsoever things are lovely, whatsoever things are of good report; if there be any virtue, and if there be any praise, think on these things.

Philippians 4:8 NKJV

But the Comforter, which is the Holy Ghost, whom the Father will send in my name, he shall teach you all things, and bring all things to your remembrance, whatsoever I have said unto you.

John 14:26 KJV

Let this mind be in you, which was also in Christ Jesus

Philippians 2:5 NKJV

MY MS JOURNEY PRAYER

Lord, I humbly ask you to rescue me from my cognitive, memory, and emotional difficulties. The adversary has come to steal, kill, and destroy my health and well-being, but I am grateful that Jesus came to bring abundant life. I fervently pray that my spirit, mind, and body are blessed with abundant health. I pray for the immediate healing of all disease symptoms. Thank You for coming to my aid. Amen.

MY MS JOURNEY MOTIVATIONAL THOUGHT OF THE DAY

*You alone are responsible for your own **Happiness**! If you put your **Happiness** in the hands of other people or wait for them to do it, you will inevitably be let down.*

GET UP AND KEEP IT MOVING!!!

DATE: _____

You were having a conversation with somebody, and you got off to an excellent start; however, all of a sudden, you find that you can't recall what you were saying since you were distracted by something that knocked you off focus. Have you ever found yourself in a predicament similar to that one?

_____

_____

_____

_____

_____

_____

_____

_____

_____

_____

_____

_____

_____

_____

_____

_____

_____

_____

_____

_____

_____

SURVIVING MULTIPLE SCLEROSIS

DAY FOURTEEN:

MY MS JOURNEY OF BLADDER CONTROL PROBLEMS

Lesions caused by multiple sclerosis (MS) can block or delay the transmission of nerve signals in regions of the central nervous system (CNS) that control the bladder and urinary sphincters, which can lead to bladder dysfunction. Bladder dysfunction affects at least 80 percent of persons who have MS. The following are examples of symptoms that may be caused by a spastic (overactive) bladder that is unable to hold the normal amount of urine, or a bladder that does not empty properly and retains some urine in it: Frequency and/or urgency of urination, leakage of urine when urinating, and/or urinary infections. Inability to completely empty the bladder, hesitancy when starting to urinate, frequent urinating throughout the night, incontinence which is the inability to hold in urine, and incontinence are all symptoms of overactive bladder.

*Having bladder troubles have been quite challenging. It's possible for me to be having a good time but still feel the need to go to the restroom. If I have to go, there is no waiting, and if I wait or if I can't get to where I need to be, there is a chance that I will be involved in an accident. On multiple occasions, I have changed the clothes that I was wearing without letting anyone know the reason why. The expression **"Gotta Go, Gotta Go, Gotta Go Right NOW"** is one that I practically live by. When it comes to coping with bladder control, I don't know if anyone who is reading this has been* *suffering in silence because they were too embarrassed to tell their story. Please have compassion for yourself and realize that you are not fighting this war alone.*

There are numerous physicians working with me. I make regular visits to a urologist to check on the health of my bladder and make sure it is emptying properly. My kidneys have been giving me problems, and my doctor is keeping a close eye on them. I just wanted to convey that there have been multiple situations where there has been blood in my urine. In order to figure out what's wrong with me, I've had blood tests, ultrasounds, and MRIs done. I have a cyst on one of my kidneys, which might be a problem, but my doctors and I are working together to make sure everything is well. It has gotten to the point where I am so worn out from the numerous problems that I have to deal with. There are a lot of people who are clueless about the struggles that other people go through in private. Disease of the kidneys is a very significant problem. I am not suggesting that I have a problem in either of my kidneys, but multiple sclerosis has damaged both my bladder and my kidneys. I just make sure that I see my doctors often and that I follow their instructions regarding my treatment. Despite the fact that this is a really difficult circumstance, I have been able to keep going with the help of prayer and support.

Those who struggle with MS or any other condition that affects their ability to control their bladder should be aware that there are exercises and medications that can help.

MY MS JOURNEY SCRIPTURE

The Lord will sustain him upon his sickbed; In his illness, you restore him to health.

Psalm 41:3 NASB

MY MS JOURNEY PRAYER

Dear Lord, today I humbly ask you to restore me to full strength and to bless me with good health. My bladder has been giving me a lot of trouble as of late. Please bless those who are taking care of me and grant me patience, tranquility, and strength at this difficult time. I am aware that you have already handled this matter. I aspire to be more like you; please assist me in becoming more like you. In the name of your Son, who is the holiest and most valuable of all, I pray. Amen

MY MS JOURNEY MOTIVATIONAL THOUGHT OF THE DAY

*I am aware that things are **challenging** for you right now, but I also am aware that **<u>YOU</u>** have what it takes to get through this!*

DATE: _____

Urine incontinence makes you feel ashamed, and as a result, you avoid participating in activities that are essential to you. You frequently get the urgent urge to urinate and run to the bathroom, but there are occasions when you are unable to make it there in time and may have an accident. How are you managing daily with these challenging issues?

_____

_____

_____

_____

_____

_____

_____

_____

_____

_____

_____

_____

_____

_____

_____

_____

_____

_____

_____

_____

SURVIVING MULTIPLE SCLEROSIS

DAY FIFTEEN:

MY MS JOURNEY OF MUSCLE SPASMS

The majority of persons who have multiple sclerosis will, at some point during the progression of their condition, report feeling some kind of discomfort or pain. MS patients often experience pain in the form of muscle spasms. This is a specific sort of cramp that might affect some individuals. **Muscle Spasms** *are a common symptom of multiple sclerosis and can show very early on in the progression of the disease, sometimes even before a diagnosis is obtained. Because they can occur at any time, muscle spasms and cramps are both frustrating and dangerous for the patient who is experiencing them. There are two possible outcomes that can take place when a muscular spasm takes place. A sudden tic or twitch may be the result of an involuntary movement of the muscle. There is also the possibility of the muscle completely contracting and becoming rigid, much like a sudden paralysis or a total cramp. Both forms of muscular spasms have the potential to cause excruciating agony.*

The process of demyelination that takes place over the course of the neurological disease can be the root cause of muscle spasms. Demyelination is a condition that can develop if the myelin coating that surrounds and protects nerves is damaged. This might cause a disruption in the impulses that are conveyed throughout the neurological system, which can result in spasms and cramps in the muscles. These particular issues can also be caused by lesions that are present on the brain or the spinal cord, which might exert pressure on particular regions. Testing with an MRI can be helpful in determining whether or not certain parts of the body that are causing issues have lesions or nerve damage.

A ***muscular spasm*** *can strike me at any time, no matter where I am or what I'm doing, and cause me to experience the most excruciating pain. My foot will actually twist, and once it does that, it will be literally stuck and unable to move. My hands also suffer from muscle spasms at times. In addition, I suffer from muscle spasms in my abdomen, which are referred to as an MS hug. An MS hug, also known as banding or girdling, is a sensation of pressure that wraps around the chest or abdomen. The embrace causes a certain kind of nerve discomfort. Additionally, I deal with the Lhermitte syndrome, often known as the barber chair phenomenon, which is frequently related with multiple sclerosis (MS). When you bend your neck, you may experience a quick and unpleasant sensation that runs down your spine from your neck all the way to your lower back. The symptoms of Lhermitte's disease are frequently compared as an electric shock or buzzing sensation. My legs start to buzz after I've been walking for some distance.*

I'm not exaggerating when I say that this has been the most excruciating experience I've ever had to go through in my entire life. Dealing with the pain and not knowing what the future holds due to this disease is really challenging. I just push through the discomfort and keep moving forward. There are moments when all I can do is cry, pray, and believe God daily for my healing. As a result of going through this process, I have come to the conclusion that there is a point in each of our lives when we have to push through the pain and acknowledge that there is a hope that exists at the end of our journey.

MY MS JOURNEY SCRIPTURE

And God shall wipe away all tears from their eyes; and there shall be no more death, neither sorrow, nor crying, neither shall there be any more pain: for the former things are passed away.

Revelation 21:4 KJV

He healeth the broken in heart, and bindeth up their wounds. He telleth the number of the stars; he calleth them all by their names. Great is our Lord, and of great power: his understanding is infinite.

Psalm 147:3-5 KJV

MY MS JOURNEY PRAYER

Lord, the God of Peace I find solace in the knowledge that, despite the pain I am experiencing, I have not disregarded the guidance of the Most Holy One. I continue to rely on Your word and the truth that you have provided. I am grateful to You for keeping me and for allowing me to persevere through my pain. I will be delivered from the pain that I am experiencing. Because You are my Most Awesome Healer, I hereby decree that I will experience healing and freedom from pain in this life. Amen.

MY MS JOURNEY MOTIVATIONAL THOUGHT OF THE DAY

__PAIN__ that lasts for an extended period of time can cause damage on multiple levels, including the mental, emotional, and spiritual ones. Try to keep in mind that, despite the fact that it hurts, we should __PRAY__ that the pain won't remain __FOREVER!__

A muscle spasm can occur in any muscle in the body, including skeletal muscles and smooth muscles, such as those found in the calf, back, thigh, or hand, among other places. In the event that you get sudden muscle spasms, what treatment methods do you use?

_____

_____

_____

_____

_____

_____

_____

_____

_____

_____

_____

_____

_____

_____

_____

_____

_____

SURVIVING MULTIPLE SCLEROSIS

MY MS JOURNEY OF EVERY 6 MONTHS "INFUSIONS, MRI'S AND BLOOD WORK"

*Because of my multiple sclerosis (MS), I need to receive **infusions every six months.** I can tell without a doubt that I felt a great deal of fear when I was first informed that I would need to undergo infusions twice every six months. Multiple sclerosis is treated with a wide variety of drugs. Rituximab was the drug that was suggested by my physician. Infusion of Rituxan is done intravenously (IV), and it is performed by a trained medical expert. The anti-cancer medication known as Rituxan works by inhibiting the expansion and dissemination of cancer cells throughout the body. It is also used to treat a variety of illnesses that are not cancers. My physician spent some time walking me through the process of how the medicine works, the potential adverse effects, and the rationale for why I needed to take the medication. The drug lessens the severity of the disease's symptoms and delays its progression. It does not reverse the condition, but it does decrease the disease's progression. MS is a degenerative disease, yet despite the progression of my condition, I have learned to believe in God. When I first started getting MRIs, I had to get them once every three months, but now I just get them every six months.*

During the course of my going through the diagnostic procedures to determine what was wrong with me. I had to have blood drawn, a spinal tap performed, as well as MRIs of both my brain and spine. If anyone has ever had a spinal tap performed on them. All I can say is **My God, My God, My God.** *My MRI showed that I have damage on both my brain and my spine, and the results of my blood work were positive. After completing all of the necessary tests, my primary care physician shared the news with me that I have multiple sclerosis (MS) during my appointment. The results of every test pointed to multiple sclerosis being the underlying condition. I was in such extreme distress when I learned the news that I really went into shock. My only thought was that I was going to* **DIE,** *and I also entertained the thought that I would become blind, bedridden, or confined to a wheelchair. The things that were going through my head at the time I reflected on the past in order to try to piece together how this illness could have been my diagnosis. I have no idea where this disease came from, but what I do know for sure is that it is not new in any way. I believe I have had MS since a child. All the symptoms I dealt with as a child I still deal with as an adult but worse. In order for the doctor to evaluate where my levels are, she requires that I submit to a blood draw every six months in advance of receiving my infusions in order to establish the appropriate number of doses to administer. In the event that my levels are high, I will require two separate infusions. If my current levels remain stable, I will be given one. Since I was first diagnosed, I've had an infusion every six months for a total of two. I receive MRI scans every six months; to check for any new lesions that may have developed on my brain or spine. This will also assess the* *locations of the MS as well as its degree of progression.* **Help Lord, Help!!!!**

MY MS JOURNEY SCRIPTURE

And he said unto them, this is my blood of the New Testament, which is shed for many.

Mark 14:24 KJV

MY MS JOURNEY PRAYER

You are the God who performs miracles. Please create an image for me of what my version of freedom might look like. Help me have the faith to believe in You so that I might receive my miracle. Show me what causes me to feel exhausted. Show me what controls me and causes me to move more slowly. Please assist me in overcoming my preference for things that make me weaker and developing a desire for things that make me stronger. Make me whole on the inside and out! Please assist me in making the required changes. I want You to be a part of the healing process that I am going through. Awaken in me a new and vibrant life! In Jesus Name Amen

MY MS JOURNEY MOTIVATIONAL THOUGHT OF THE DAY

*This is **Challenging,** but you can **Overcome** it because you're more **Powerful!***

88

DATE: _____

Even though the procedure is difficult, you will be able to get through this. Although it might be very overwhelming to have MRIs and bloodwork done every six months, you should try to remain positive and take things one day at a time. You should try to remind yourself of three positive statements every day by writing them down and repeating them until you start to believe them.

_____

_____

_____

_____

_____

_____

_____

_____

_____

_____

_____

_____

_____

_____

_____

_____

MY MS JOURNEY OF UNKNOWN "MS FLARE-UPS"

My own experience has taught me that flare-ups of multiple sclerosis are similar to sneak attacks; they occur at times when you are least prepared for them. It has been brought to my attention that you could be aware of the attacks at this point. You need to have a solid awareness of your body, in addition to being aware of the factors that tend to stress you out and the things that set you off. If you find yourself in a position similar to this one, it is absolutely necessary for you to take precautions to protect your health. Be aware of the attacks that are happening. They could appear or they could not, but you have to make sure that you are getting enough rest, eating well, taking your medication as directed, and attending all of your regular appointments in case they do. You should also avoid taking on anybody else's problems in addition to your own. You are responsible for making sure that you are well protected and that you take good care of yourself at all times.

I had my first MS attack/MS flare-up June 26, 2021. *I need to go back to when the symptoms (mention stroke 2017) and I didn't understand what was going on in my body dealing with numbness, weakness, couldn't feel my body from my chest to my feet. It was so bad that I couldn't walk. I went to the ER during the pandemic alone. That was a scary time to be alone not knowing what was going on. I had to go through a battery of testing before it was determined that*

I had an MS attack. According to the findings of my MRI scan, I recently acquired a new lesion on my spinal cord, which was the root cause of the relapse. This attack landed me in the hospital for 5 days having to get aggressive treatment of steroids and other medications. I had to spend every day in the hospital by myself, taking this powerful medication, and had needles inserted into my stomach on a daily basis in order to prevent the formation of a blood clot because I couldn't walk. Doctors coming in every morning to evaluate my progress. Listen, I was in so much fear that all I could do was pray and cry since I had no idea what the conclusion would be. Because of my mobility issues, I have to either use a wheelchair, walker or walk around walls in order to move around.

*   **Flare-ups of multiple sclerosis**, despite the fact that they are unpredictable and depressing, may be something that you learn to live with over time. In my experience, it is not always simple to determine whether an increase in the severity of already present symptoms or the appearance of brand-new symptoms is the result of a relapse or whether it is instead the result of another cause, such as an infection, stress, or simply spending too much time in the sun. This is because there are a number of factors that can contribute to the manifestation of these symptoms. **MS flare-ups are not fun!** They frequently developed out of nowhere and could continue for several days at a time. When you are in such a state of intense fatigue, it is impossible to engage in any kind of activity. Regardless of how I might be physically feeling at any given moment, I am the*

kind of person who has to always have something to keep me occupied. My years of living with multiple sclerosis have provided me with the opportunity to experience the incapacitating exhaustion that frequently accompanies a relapse. This has allowed me to better understand and empathize with those who are in this position. If you are not careful, these factors may prevent you from accomplishing your goals of getting the most out of life and experiencing it to the fullest.

MY MS JOURNEY SCRIPTURE

Peace, I leave with you; my peace I give you. I do not give to you as the world gives. Do not let your hearts be troubled and do not be afraid.

John 14:27 NIV

Even though I walk through the darkest valley, I will fear no evil, for you are with me; your rod and your staff, they comfort me.

Psalms 23:4 NIV

MY MS JOURNEY PRAYER

My God, the challenges I faced today felt like they were too much for me to handle. And then there will be more of the same things, in addition to perhaps some brand new, difficulties, when I wake up tomorrow. I require the power that you provide. I can't go through the storms of life without You supporting me and standing by my side. It's that I've never fully realized how literally your vows to strengthen us for the day are meant to be taken. I have complete confidence in the infinite power that originates from within you. I am grateful that despite my frailties, You, have worked in them and invested Your strength in me. Perhaps tomorrow will present me with the chance to get a more profound understanding of what that expression implies. But right now, I am asking for divine power and healing to infiltrate every cell of my being so that I can discover a revitalized strength that is beyond what is possible with my natural abilities. I have no doubt that You are the source of my strength. In Jesus' name, amen.

MY MS JOURNEY MOTIVATIONAL THOUGHT OF THE DAY

*A multiple sclerosis **flare up** can come on without warning and it can occur at any time. Sometimes it's not always necessary to have a plan. Sometimes all you need to do is take a few deep breaths, place your **Trust** in the **Spiritual Realm,** and **Let Go**!*

Through Christ, who strengthens me, I am able to accomplish all things!!

DATE: _____

When you have multiple sclerosis, it might be challenging to maintain a consistent daily schedule at times. The challenges of daily living can be difficult enough, but larger, more upsetting events in one's life can make MS flares worse. What strategies do you use to deal with the stresses of your daily life?

_____

_____

_____

_____

_____

_____

_____

_____

_____

_____

_____

_____

_____

_____

_____

_____

_____

_____

_____

SURVIVING MULTIPLE SCLEROSIS

DAY EIGHTEEN:

MY MS JOURNEY OF LOSS OF BALANCE "FALLING"

People who have multiple sclerosis frequently have issues with their gait, which manifests itself as difficulty walking. In actuality, this is one of the most typical difficulties with mobility that people who have multiple sclerosis experience. Maintaining one's muscle strength and flexibility is best accomplished by engaging in physical therapy, performing regular exercise, or stretching regularly. People typically discover that increasing their muscle strength, particularly in the core, can also assist them improve their balance.

*According to study that was carried out in a number of different countries, between 50 and 70 percent of people who have Multiple Sclerosis have indicated that they have experienced a fall during the most recent two to six months. A little less than a third of those individuals claim that they have experienced multiple falls, with injuries resulting directly from the occurrences themselves. It is of the utmost importance to enhance a person's walking abilities so that they can do so in a secure and pleasant manner while also lowering their danger of falling. Not only does falling have the potential to inflict injuries, but the length of time necessary to recuperate from broken bones or strained muscles can exacerbate mobility concerns and lower degrees of independence. Falls can cause injury. **People who have multiple sclerosis are at an increased risk of falling,** and these accidents frequently take place* in or around the areas where they live, such as their houses or neighborhoods. The majority of the time, these mishaps happen when people are going about their daily activities, such as taking a shower, preparing meals, or navigating crowded areas. **It is impossible to generalize about the elements that contribute to an increased risk of falling because they vary from person to person.**

This is a specific area to focus on. I can say with complete honesty that I have endured a number of falls, each of which has left me in severe pain and, but for the **Grace of God**, could have resulted in my death. Because there have been so many of them that I can't even count them on one hand. There have been so many of them that I have lost track of how many times I have fallen down the stairs. The fall that left me with a concussion and a significant injury to my leg. I was getting ready to leave for Jamaica in order to attend the wedding of my cousin there. I finished my lunch at the office, and then I walked to the mall to return an item of clothing. There were cracks in the ground and the foundation of the walls within the entryway where I was walking when I was walking up to the mall to access it. It wasn't until my heel became caught that I realized what was going on, and by the time I did, I had already twisted my ankle, fallen forward trying to regain my balance, and struck my head on the glass window. I give thanks to God that it was a double pain glass because if it hadn't been a double pain glass, the doctors in the emergency room told me that there was a good chance that I would not be here today. In addition, I had to get stitches since I had cut my knee wide open and torn some of the ligaments in my knee. To name just a few, I had a significant fall down the stairs at my home, which resulted in my slamming my head on the front door and injuring my arms trying to stop myself from falling. This was just one of many accidents that have happened to me. I recently slipped while climbing the stairs while carrying a cup of hot tea, and as a result, I burned my left hand, which has left a permanent mark on it. **Help me, Lord, I've been knocked down and I can't get up!** I can tell with all sincerity that I am exhausted from constantly stumbling and falling down. It makes sense, given that you have multiple sclerosis (MS), that you would experience that. I have been trying to be more conscious of my environment and have become more aware as a result of a number of falls.

Pay attention to the stairs that lead up to you rather than the entire staircase!

MY MS JOURNEY SCRIPTURE
Have mercy on me, O LORD, for I am weak; O LORD, heal me, for my bones are troubled.

Psalms 6:2 KJV

MY MS JOURNEY PRAYER
Dear Lord, I ask you to provide me a robust immune system so that I can put up a good fight against bacterial and viral illnesses. Please hear my prayer. I give You thanks that when You created me, you also developed this defense mechanism inside of me to

prevent me from getting sick. I need your help to be attentive in promoting a strong immune system through healthy habits and avoiding behaviors that weaken it. Please hear my prayer. Amen.

MY MS JOURNEY MOTIVATIONAL THOUGHT OF THE DAY

*Keep in mind that you need to **Maintain Your Focus** despite the difficulties you may have. On the other hand, in order to make any progress in comprehending what came before, one must continually **Look Forward**!*

DATE: _____

People who have trouble maintaining their equilibrium could have the impression that they are moving even when they are not moving at all. It's possible that they'll experience shaky legs or a sensation that the world around them is spinning. They might have feelings of confusion or disorientation, which could cause them to lose their balance and their awareness of their surroundings. How do you manage your frailty, prevent yourself from losing your balance, and lessen the likelihood that you will fall?

_____

_____

_____

_____

_____

_____

_____

_____

_____

_____

_____

_____

_____

_____

_____

SURVIVING MULTIPLE SCLEROSIS

DAY NINETEEN:

MY MS JOURNEY OF VISION PROBLEMS "LORD OPEN MY EYES"

For many individuals suffering from multiple sclerosis, one of the first signs of the disease is an issue with your eyesight. **Vision issues are a potentially relapsing symptom of multiple sclerosis (MS).** *They could only affect one of your eyes or both of them. The issues may become more severe before going away entirely, or they may continue to exist. If you are aware of the different kinds of visual disturbances that could affect you, you will be better prepared to deal with them in the event that they become permanent. Multiple sclerosis frequently results in a variety of visual symptoms, including double vision, involuntary movements, blindness, and optic neuritis. Although vision problems in MS patients might not be able to be avoided entirely, there are activities that can be taken to assist prevent or lessen the likelihood that vision problems will emerge. Taking frequent breaks to give your eyes a rest during the course of the day can help avoid an upcoming flare-up or minimize the severity of an existing one. Visual disturbances can be less severe and long-term harm can be prevented if they are diagnosed and treated in a timely manner.*

My God, there are so many distinct aspects to this disease, and each one has the potential to affect you in a different way. That is why I continue to meditate on his word and pray continually for healing. I make it a point to obtain annual eye exams to check and see whether the disease has had any impact on my vision. I have to be honest and tell that I do have issues with my vision, but all that I require at this moment are reading glasses. My nighttime driving is a complete disaster. Especially when the headlights of other vehicles shine in my eyes, it's difficult for me to see well. As time goes my eyes are becoming worse. Concerning my diagnosis and everything that comes along with it, I pray constantly. I also pray that the Lord will open my eyes to what I need to do and to move forward without thinking about what could possibly happen but rather to live in the now knowing that **life is too short to not enjoy every day that you get up and open your eyes.** This is not even close to being an easy journey. However, as one gains experience, every new day presents new opportunities. Let me see as the blind man saw when Jesus reopened his eyes, Lord Jesus. All that is around me should be brought to my attention through my five senses. Please help me get closer to you with all that I encounter.

MY MS JOURNEY SCRIPTURE

Open my eyes so that I will observe amazing things from your instruction.

Psalm 119:18 ISV

Then Jesus laid his hands on his eyes again; and he opened his eyes, his sight was restored, and he saw everything clearly.

Matthew 8:25 ESV

MY MS JOURNEY PRAYER

Lord, please enlighten my eyes, heart, mind, and hands! Lord, open the eyes of my heart! Please open my eyes to see what you want me to see. Please open my ears to hear you clearly when you speak. Please allow me to accept from you by opening my heart. Please allow me to love like you do. Please help me understand by opening my thoughts this will help me hear clearly from you. Please extend your hands to me so that I may get the assistance you are so ready to provide. Please allow me to share your goodness with others boldly, freely, and passionately.

Please grant me a greater passion for the lost but please, Lord, give me an undeniable burden for souls, a passion and compassion for people! Please guide me in entirely trusting you, completely obeying you, and completely following you wherever you may lead, knowing that I will always find perfect joy and tranquility at the center of your will!

In Jesus Name Amen!

MY MS JOURNEY MOTIVATIONAL THOUGHT OF THE DAY

__Lord,__ I need your help to make sure that __I__ never forget to keep my eyes focused on __YOU__ no matter what!

DATE: _____

Having issues with one's vision can be a very unsettling experience. What steps are you taking to correct any vision challenges so that you can avoid major long-term problems?

_____

_____

_____

_____

_____

_____

_____

_____

_____

_____

_____

_____

_____

_____

_____

_____

_____

_____

SURVIVING MULTIPLE SCLEROSIS

MY MS JOURNEY OF TRAUMA & GRIEF
MY THERAPEUTIC COUNSELING JOURNEY

Grief *is a feeling that each of us will, at some point in our lives, experience, and it has the potential to be one of the most terrible and life-changing events that we will ever go through.* **Grief can be caused by a variety of events, including unexpected medical diagnoses, the loss of a job, or the end of a relationship; however, death is the most common cause.** *The particulars of a person's life at the time of their loss or traumatic experience have a significant bearing on the intensity and breadth of the impact that sorrow has on that person's life. Grief affects each and every one of us in a way that is singular to our histories and to the identities that we have established for ourselves as individuals. As a result of this, there is no correct or incorrect way to grieve; rather, it is simply an element of who we are.*

Since I first started going to therapy, the experience has completely transformed my life. After learning that I have multiple sclerosis, I went through a period in which I struggled with feelings of depression, fear, stress, and worry. I had the feeling that no one believed me, and that I was alone going through this. My time spent in therapy has not only helped me work through challenging life decisions and challenging situations, but it has also shown me how to have a better understanding of myself, including my diagnosis, my worries, my stressors, and my fears, and how to put my attention on my own personal growth and wellness.

This was due to the fact that counseling led me step-by-step through the process of making changes in my life and understanding MS for myself. The practice of writing in and maintaining a journal as part of a healing process has a long and important history. Through my experiences, I have come to understand that no one but you can control the level of happiness you experience in your life. When you put your happiness in the hands of other people or wait for them to make you happy, you are setting yourself up to be disappointed in the end.

Please keep in mind that traveling down this road by oneself is not an easy task. Please look for someone who is able to assist you through this difficult time if you feel that you need help. It's important and has the potential to completely transform your life! You will be able to move on and arrive at the place you need to be in order to go forward in a way that brings you healing and peace!!!

I owe a tremendous amount of gratitude to my _**Therapist**_ for all of her insight, expertise, and compassion in assisting me in being more confident in myself and navigating the challenges of my journey with MS. Believe me when I say that if therapy has benefited me, then I am certain beyond a reasonable doubt that it will assist you as well. Try it out for yourself instead of listening to what other *people have to say about it or being distracted by what they may think about therapy.*

MY MS JOURNEY SCRIPTURE

Peace is what I leave with you; it is my own peace that I give you. I do not give it as the world does. Do not be worried and upset; do not be afraid.

John 14:27 GNT

The Lord is my Rock, my fortress, my place of safety. He is my God, the Rock I run to for protection. He is my shield; by his power I am saved. He is my hiding place high in the hills.

Psalm 18:2 ERV

The LORD himself goes before you and will be with you; he will never leave you nor forsake you. Do not be afraid; do not be discouraged."

Deuteronomy 31:8 NIV

MY MS JOURNEY PRAYER

Lord, I pray that you will send healing. In the middle of all the suffering, provide peace. In the midst of hopelessness, you will offer encouragement. Because I am incapable of navigating this valley on my own, I pray that You will bestow upon me the necessary strength to do so. I simply cannot comprehend that there will be happier times ahead. Assist me in overcoming this challenge so that I might emerge on the other side more powerful; yet, for the time being, please hold on to me tightly amid the pain. In Jesus' name, Amen.

MY MS JOURNEY MOTIVATIONAL THOUGHT OF THE DAY

The Achievement of One Success does not Guarantee Another!

*The **foundation** of it is **defeat**. **Frustration** serves as the foundation for it. There are occasions when it is constructed on a **Catastrophe**. People become more **Resilient** after experiencing adversity.*

DATE: _____

Where is the pain? Within your very being? What are some things that, when thought about or discussed, can make you feel sad? Who exactly are you discussing this matter with? What kind of assistance do they provide? Who do you think you could trust?

_____

_____

_____

_____

_____

_____

_____

_____

_____

_____

_____

_____

_____

_____

_____

_____

_____

_____

_____

SURVIVING MULTIPLE SCLEROSIS

DAY TWENTY-ONE:

MY MS JOURNEY OF SELF-CARE

Practicing **self-care** implies acknowledging and emphasizing the relationship we have with ourselves; hence, in order to keep this relationship healthy, we must make a conscientious effort to maintain it. There are times when it requires us to call ourselves out on the things that we are doing that aren't good for our health. When I wake up in the morning, I have a newfound appreciation for life and the significance of looking after myself. I had to adjust the way I thought about myself and the obligations I have in life. I became aware of how vital it is for me to appreciate the fact that I am here today and to make sure that I take care of myself. I have found that going to a significant and secluded location where I may pray, contemplate, and seek God's will for my life is really beneficial. I drive to the beach, park my car, and sit there to observe the sea, the birds, and the people who are there. Taking care of yourself should be one of your top priorities in life. I just went about my day like normal and didn't bother to take care of myself at all. I had no idea that I was neglecting my own needs while attending to those of others. One thing about me is that I am able to offer everyone else ideas, advice, and recommendations that will help them improve themselves, but what about you and what about me?

Nothing should be taken for granted. It is our responsibility to demonstrate love and kindness to people whose lives intersect or run parallel to ours while we are on this earth because we do not know when our next breath will be our last. Carry it out. Be kind. Practice kindness and compassion, first with yourself and then with others. Participate in activities offered by the Multiple Sclerosis Society on the regional, state, or national level. On Facebook, they have some amazing chat groups, and there are always individuals who are willing to talk you through whatever is going on in your life.

YOU HAVE THIS UNDER CONTROL!

When we give more of our time to God, He will refresh us, give us new strength, and remind us that we do not have to face the challenges of life on our own. We are not alone, and God will give us whatever we require to fulfill the assignment that he has entrusted to us. Today, I want to urge you to make time in your schedule to spend with God in prayer and thankfulness, staying connected with him so that you can gain better insight and direction.

Because of this, God did not give us the spirit of fear, but rather the Spirit of Strength, Love, and Self-Control!

MY MS JOURNEY SCRIPTURE
A cheerful disposition is good for your health; gloom and doom leave you bone tired.

Proverbs 17:22 MSG

Very early in the morning, while it was still dark, Jesus got up, left the house, and went off to a solitary place, where he prayed.

Mark 1:35 NIV

MY MS JOURNEY PRAYER

Please, Lord, make me worthy of receiving Your benefits today. I ask that you bless me with courage and grant me the ability to focus on myself today, tomorrow, and for the rest of my life. I humbly ask that you grant me with the wisdom of patience and knowledge. I ask that throughout the day, you will strengthen me to make the decisions that will allow me to walk boldly and operate in an appropriate manner. In Your name, I pray for each and every one of these things. Amen.

MY MS JOURNEY MOTIVATIONAL THOUGHT OF THE DAY

*It is not **necessary** to view the **entire staircase**; all you need to do is take the **first step**!*

__SELF-CARE__ is the means by which one reclaims __POWER__!!!

__SELF-LOVE__ is the most important kind of __LOVE__!!!

__TAKE CARE OF YOUR SELF!!!__

DATE: _____

It is absolutely essential to the outcome of your healing process that you prioritize taking care of yourself. I've discovered that the process of taking care of myself involves working on our physical, spiritual, and emotional health, all of which are truly connected to one another and support one another. This is something that I've found to be true. Make a list of the things you can do to take care of yourself, considering any and all factors that could affect the likelihood that you will remain healthy.

_____

_____

_____

_____

_____

_____

_____

_____

_____

_____

_____

_____

_____

_____

_____

SURVIVING MULTIPLE SCLEROSIS

DAY TWENTY-TWO:

MY MS JOURNEY OF FINISH STRONG

Finishing Strong is an important part of the healing process. It is the attitude of believing in yourself and having the courage and determination to see something through to completion. Commitment, integrity, and excellence are all aspects of remembering who you are while healing. Say a simple motivating sentence aloud every day as soon as you get out of bed. I understand how important it is to stay motivated during difficult times in life. I read this inspiring scripture every morning before I start my day. **Philippians 4:13 says, "I can do all things through Christ who strengthens me."** God provides us with everything we require to endure adversity, including health, wealth, and wisdom.

I had a good talk with God one day when I was upset about being diagnosed with Multiple Sclerosis. I literally heard a small voice tell me that you are a gift. I said, "Wait, what a gift, stop playing," because it didn't make sense to me. I then opened the Bible to Proverbs 18:16, a powerful statement that revealed the answer to my Why Me! "A man's gift makes room for him" God has given each person a gift or talent that the world will accommodate. The gift God has given you will allow you to realize your vision. It will pave the way for you to **"Live in Freedom Everyday"** in life. Yes, this journey is difficult for me to comprehend, but **I STILL**

BELIEVE GOD! *God will give you the strength to fight every battle, the wisdom to make every decision, and the peace that surpasses all knowledge and understanding. Remember to* **Finish Strong Every Day**, *regardless of how you feel, what you've been through, what you've been told, what you may have lost, or how you're dealing with the fear of it all. It is not important where you begin; rather, what matters is where you end up.*

MY MS JOURNEY SCRIPTURE

Have not I commanded thee? Be strong and of a good courage; be not afraid, neither be thou dismayed: for the LORD thy God is with thee whithersoever thou goest.

Joshua 1:9 KJV

Beloved, I wish above all things that you may prosper and be in health, even as your soul prospers.

3 John 1:2 KJV

Let us not become weary in doing good, for at the proper time we will reap a harvest if we do not give up.

Galatians 6:9 NIV

MY MS JOURNEY PRAYER

You are the God of all things miraculous. Please paint a picture for me of what my version of freedom might look like. Help me have the faith to believe in You so that I might receive my miracle. Show me what causes me to feel exhausted. Show me what controls me and causes me to move more slowly. Please assist me in getting rid of the desire I have for things that bring me down and developing a preference for things that build me up. Make me whole on the inside and out! Please grant me peaceful acceptance of what I can't alter, courageous action on what I can, and the discernment to know the difference are all things I pray for. Please assist me in making the required adjustments. I desire that You be part of the healing process that I am going through. Father, please grant me a new lease on life while I'm on this journey! In Jesus' Name, Amen.

MY MS JOURNEY MOTIVATIONAL THOUGHT OF THE DAY

Be true to who **YOU** are and express how **YOU** truly feel, since the people who **MATTER** won't mind, and the people who **MIND** won't **MATTER!**

Please do not forget to:

FINISH STRONG EVERYDAY!

DATE: _____

We are aware that things aren't always simple, but you have to remember to maintain your focus, keep moving forward, and not let the circumstances you find yourself in bring you down. Never surrender on something you have faith in, and never listen to anyone who tells you that you can't accomplish something. If you could put down three goals that you want to achieve in the next three months, what would they be?

_____

_____

_____

_____

_____

_____

_____

_____

_____

_____

_____

_____

_____

_____

_____

_____

_____

_____

SURVIVING MULTIPLE SCLEROSIS

The next chapter of this book is for you to spend some time writing about your own journey through life after I have shared with you several aspects of my experience living with multiple sclerosis (MS). In spite of the fact that I have been diagnosed with multiple sclerosis, you might be interested in writing about a different illness, testimonial, or experience. From my own personal experience, I've found that putting thoughts and ideas down on paper is the most efficient way to break free of a difficult situation or issue. You won't have to worry about anyone else's reaction to what you've told them or how they might feel about what you've shared with them if you write down your thoughts, feelings, and concerns and keep them in a safe place. If you do this, you'll have peace of mind. There is a powerful statement that has helped me move forward in my life without contemplating what other people may think of me or the circumstances I find myself in.

Take a look at this powerful statement:

"It makes no difference what other people think; the only thing that matters is what God has to say!

The process of writing is essential to your own growth and development. There are some people who are unable to communicate themselves through conversation but keeping a journal of your journey is a way that you can express yourself. **Make sure you give yourself enough time to navigate through your** *journey!* *When you are carrying heavy burdens that are dragging you down, it is quite difficult to maneuver through life. Take the time to write out your own personal journey in order to free yourself of the burdens that are holding you back. You are about to embark on a journey of your own, and here is a personal journal for you to use for the next 30 days. You will find a means to express yourself here that is unrestricted and free from any critical feedback, remarks, or suggestions from other people. Simply a means for you to communicate your thoughts and feelings with God. Writing in a journal gives you the opportunity to get all of the words, thoughts, and frustrations running through your head down on paper. When they are committed to paper, they take on a more concrete form. Come back in a few hours and go over what you wrote with a fresh pair of eyes. It's possible that you won't believe how differently you feel after this. In addition, you may go back and read previous entries in your journal to see how your thoughts have evolved over time.*

*There is a motivating phrase waiting for you at the beginning of each and every one of your individual experiences to get you excited about the journey you are about to go on and to continue getting you excited about it. It is important to remember that this is **your journey**. Just focus on getting through today! Writing gives you the freedom to express yourself! I don't know how bad things look for you right now but please hear me out, life is just so short, there isn't enough time in the day to worry about any of it. At this very* *moment, God is working on you. There is always a purpose behind the actions you take in your life. By thinking back on your life, you can gain a better understanding of who you are and the reasons you are still here. Find out what it is and make it all the way through your journey successfully! It is important to remember that this is* **YOUR JOURNEY!!!**

Remember simply concentrate on making it through today! The ability to express oneself freely through writing is a wonderful thing!

NAVIGATE YOUR WAY THROUGH YOUR JOURNEY!

LET'S BEGIN

"For I know the plans I have for you," says the LORD. "They are plans for good and not for disaster, to give you a future and a hope."

Jeremiah 29:11 NIV

DAY ONE

Outside of one's comfort zone is where all progress takes place!

Date:_____

My Personal Journey With: _____

_____

_____

_____

_____

_____

_____

_____

_____

_____

_____

_____

_____

_____

_____

_____

_____

_____

_____

_____

_____

SURVIVING MY JOURNEY

DAY TWO

I refuse to entertain any thoughts that are filled with uncertainty, anxiety, or discouragement!

Date:_____

My Personal Journey With: _____

_____

_____

_____

_____

_____

_____

_____

_____

_____

_____

_____

_____

_____

_____

_____

_____

_____

_____

_____

_____

_____

SURVIVING MY JOURNEY

DAY THREE

I command all of the angels who serve the Lord to remove every obstacle that stands in the way of the full manifestation of my breakthrough!

Date:_____

My Personal Journey With: _____

_____

_____

_____

_____

_____

_____

_____

_____

_____

_____

_____

_____

_____

_____

_____

_____

_____

_____

SURVIVING MY JOURNEY

DAY FOUR

Lord, I ask for your assistance in locating any areas of weakness within me that may be preventing the manifestation of my miracles, and then in overcoming those areas!

*Date:*_____

My Personal Journey With: _____

_____

_____

_____

_____

_____

_____

_____

_____

_____

_____

_____

_____

_____

_____

_____

_____

_____

_____

_____

SURVIVING MY JOURNEY

DAY FIVE

*I pray that every bad and powerful man in my life will be
disarmed and brought to ruin!*

Date:_____

My Personal Journey With:_____

_____

_____

_____

_____

_____

_____

_____

_____

_____

_____

_____

_____

_____

_____

_____

_____

_____

_____

_____

_____

_____

SURVIVING MY JOURNEY

DAY SIX

I stop every strongman who has been tasked with preventing the realization of my miracles!

*Date:*_____

My Personal Journey With: _____

_____

_____

_____

_____

_____

_____

_____

_____

_____

_____

_____

_____

_____

_____

_____

_____

_____

_____

SURVIVING MY JOURNEY

DAY SEVEN

Please, in the name of Jesus, respond to my prayer with fire because you're the God who gave Jacob a <u>New Beginning</u>!

*Date:*_____

My Personal Journey With: _____

_____

_____

_____

_____

_____

_____

_____

_____

_____

_____

_____

_____

_____

_____

_____

_____

_____

_____

SURVIVING MY JOURNEY

DAY EIGHT

In the name of Jesus, please, Lord, take swift vengeance on those who wrong me!

*Date:*_____

My Personal Journey With: _____

_____

_____

_____

_____

_____

_____

_____

_____

_____

_____

_____

_____

_____

_____

_____

_____

_____

_____

_____

SURVIVING MY JOURNEY

DAY NINE

It is not the purpose of life to discover oneself. Creating the person, you will be is the purpose of life!

Date:_____

My Personal Journey With: _____

_____

_____

_____

_____

_____

_____

_____

_____

_____

_____

_____

_____

_____

_____

_____

_____

_____

_____

_____

SURVIVING MY JOURNEY

DAY TEN

You will only ever turn out to be exactly the person you give yourself permission to be!

*Date:*_____

My Personal Journey With: _____

_____

_____

_____

_____

_____

_____

_____

_____

_____

_____

_____

_____

_____

_____

_____

_____

_____

_____

_____

SURVIVING MY JOURNEY

DAY ELEVEN

Life is a series of lessons, and in order to learn them, one must first experience them!

Date:_____

My Personal Journey With: _____

_____

_____

_____

_____

_____

_____

_____

_____

_____

_____

_____

_____

_____

_____

_____

_____

_____

_____

_____

SURVIVING MY JOURNEY

DAY TWELVE

You need to push yourself to achieve the goals you believe are out of reach!

*Date:*_____

My Personal Journey With: _____

_____

_____

_____

_____

_____

_____

_____

_____

_____

_____

_____

_____

_____

_____

_____

_____

_____

_____

_____

SURVIVING MY JOURNEY

DAY THIRTHEEN

You are never too old to dream a new dream or to pursue another goal that you have set for yourself!

Date:_____

My Personal Journey With: _____

_____

_____

_____

_____

_____

_____

_____

_____

_____

_____

_____

_____

_____

_____

_____

_____

_____

_____

_____

SURVIVING MY JOURNEY

DAY FOURTEEN

You will still make progress even if you are unsuccessful and fall flat on your face!

Date:_____

My Personal Journey With:_____

_____

_____

_____

_____

_____

_____

_____

_____

_____

_____

_____

_____

_____

_____

_____

_____

_____

_____

_____

_____

SURVIVING MY JOURNEY

DAY FIFTEEN

Act as if the things you are doing are important because they are!

Date:_____

My Personal Journey With: _____

_____

_____

_____

_____

_____

_____

_____

_____

_____

_____

_____

_____

_____

_____

_____

_____

_____

_____

SURVIVING MY JOURNEY

DAY SIXTEEN

I'd rather try to accomplish something amazing and fall short of my goal than try to accomplish nothing at all and be successful!

*Date:*_____

My Personal Journey With: _____

_____

_____

_____

_____

_____

_____

_____

_____

_____

_____

_____

_____

_____

_____

_____

_____

_____

_____

_____

SURVIVING MY JOURNEY

DAY SEVENTEEN

Continue forth even if you are going through unimaginable suffering!

Date:_____

My Personal Journey With: _____

_____

_____

_____

_____

_____

_____

_____

_____

_____

_____

_____

_____

_____

_____

_____

_____

_____

_____

_____

SURVIVING MY JOURNEY

DAY EIGHTEEN

The difficulties we face are not roadblocks but rather suggestions for improvement!

*Date:*_____

My Personal Journey With: _____

_____

_____

_____

_____

_____

_____

_____

_____

_____

_____

_____

_____

_____

_____

_____

_____

_____

_____

SURVIVING MY JOURNEY

DAY NINETEEN

We have no choice but to recognize suffering and use it as motivation for the road ahead!

Date:_____

My Personal Journey With: _____

_____

_____

_____

_____

_____

_____

_____

_____

_____

_____

_____

_____

_____

_____

_____

_____

_____

_____

SURVIVING MY JOURNEY

DAY TWENTY

No one can change what has happened in the past in order to start again, but everyone may begin anew right now and write a new chapter!

*Date:*_____

My Personal Journey With: _____

_____

_____

_____

_____

_____

_____

_____

_____

_____

_____

_____

_____

_____

_____

_____

_____

_____

_____

SURVIVING MY JOURNEY

DAY TWENTY-ONE

You shouldn't be afraid to sacrifice the excellent in order to pursue the great!

Date:_____

My Personal Journey With: _____

_____

_____

_____

_____

_____

_____

_____

_____

_____

_____

_____

_____

_____

_____

_____

_____

_____

_____

_____

_____

SURVIVING MY JOURNEY

DAY TWENTY-TWO

I'm not going to be overly critical of myself because I'm trying my absolute best!

*Date:*_____

My Personal Journey With: _____

_____

_____

_____

_____

_____

_____

_____

_____

_____

_____

_____

_____

_____

_____

_____

_____

_____

SURVIVING MY JOURNEY

DAY TWENTY-THREE

I am aware that I am equipped with the fortitude and the innate intelligence to make it through this, and I will!

Date:_____

My Personal Journey With: _____

_____

_____

_____

_____

_____

_____

_____

_____

_____

_____

_____

_____

_____

_____

_____

_____

_____

_____

_____

_____

_____

SURVIVING MY JOURNEY

DAY TWENTY-FOUR

I am confident that I will prevail despite the challenges I am facing because I have the fortitude and the innate wisdom necessary!

Date:_____

My Personal Journey With: _____

_____

_____

_____

_____

_____

_____

_____

_____

_____

_____

_____

_____

_____

_____

_____

_____

_____

_____

_____

_____

SURVIVING MY JOURNEY

DAY TWENTY-FIVE

This major life transition is stressful and challenging, but I have the ability to adjust and build an even better life for myself!

Date:_____

My Personal Journey With: _____

_____

_____

_____

_____

_____

_____

_____

_____

_____

_____

_____

_____

_____

_____

_____

_____

_____

_____

SURVIVING MY JOURNEY

DAY TWENTY-SIX

You are intelligent, strong, capable, and tenacious and you shall prevail over this challenge!

*Date:*_____

My Personal Journey With: _____

_____

_____

_____

_____

_____

_____

_____

_____

_____

_____

_____

_____

_____

_____

_____

_____

_____

_____

_____

SURVIVING MY JOURNEY

DAY TWENTY-SEVEN

Things are challenging right now, and they may be even more so tomorrow, but I'm confident that, as time goes on, they'll continue to get better!

Date:_____

My Personal Journey With: _____

_____

_____

_____

_____

_____

_____

_____

_____

_____

_____

_____

_____

_____

_____

_____

_____

_____

_____

_____

_____

_____

_____

SURVIVING MY JOURNEY

DAY TWENTY-EIGHT

Despite the fact that this circumstance is a setback, it does not define who I am. I am so much more than the things I've gone through in life!

Date:_____

My Personal Journey With: _____

_____

_____

_____

_____

_____

_____

_____

_____

_____

_____

_____

_____

_____

_____

_____

_____

_____

_____

_____

_____

SURVIVING MY JOURNEY

DAY TWENTY-NINE

When I take some time to relax and be still, I am confident that a solution will come to me!

*Date:*_____

My Personal Journey With: _____

_____

_____

_____

_____

_____

_____

_____

_____

_____

_____

_____

_____

_____

_____

_____

_____

_____

_____

SURVIVING MY JOURNEY

DAY THIRTY

I will make it through this difficult time. I shall survive the rest of this Journey. I am confident that I will get through this and come out even stronger!

Date:_____

My Personal Journey With: _____

_____

_____

_____

_____

_____

_____

_____

_____

_____

_____

_____

_____

_____

_____

_____

_____

_____

_____

SURVIVING MY JOURNEY

CLOSING

For people struggling to discover a happier, healthier way to live with this lifelong disease, it sometimes seems like an impossible task. I shared my own **challenges, frustrations, fears, anxiety, and ultimate victories** *in managing MS through daily devotion, reading, praying, motivation and journaling. This has not been an easy journey for me with multiple sclerosis, my entire life has been about giving back, from the beginning. The path that one takes through life is not always easy. It is certain that you will face challenges throughout your life; this is just the way things work. It is my prayer you received something you needed to make it through your own life's journey. Remember, as you move forward on* **YOUR JOURNEY**, *that you can't keep worrying about tomorrow because tomorrow will take care of itself regardless of what you do today. It's possible that some of the storms that come through your life are actually there to help you get to where you need to go. Instead of concentrating on the entire flight of stairs, give your full attention to the step-in front of you. So just focus on the here and now and enjoy the ride. I am well aware that it is far simpler to state than it is to put into practice, but I really believe that the best way to learn is by actual experience, and that the world itself is our instructor. Remember to keep your focus and make the most of the moments in your life. Take one step at a time, and make sure you look after yourself while you're on your journey!*

THANK YOU for taking the time to read my journey with multiple sclerosis. I pray that this book has served both as an inspiration and as a primary source of direction for you on your way to greatness, in the hopes that it will make your journey a little bit easier. Please know that you need to take one day at a time and know you are here for a **PURPOSE!**

Proverbs 4:12 NKJV states: when you walk, your steps will not be hindered, and when you run, you will not stumble! Maintain your focus, and do not look back!

That Which Is Yet to Come Is Even Better!

SUPPORTIVE RESOURCES

*The following is a list of helpful resources that can be used for gathering information, discussing your own experiences, and learning more about **Multiple Sclerosis (MS):***

National Multiple Sclerosis Society
Connecticut-Rhode Island
1111 Cromwell Ave
Suite 302C
Rocky Hill, CT 06067
Toll Free: 1-800-344-4867
www.nationalmssociety.org

"Whether you or a loved one are newly diagnosed or have had MS for many years, you have come to the right place to get connected." ("Greater Delaware Valley | National Multiple Sclerosis Society") The National MS Society is working toward a world free of MS. People affected by MS can live their best lives as we stop MS in its tracks, restore what has been lost and end MS forever.

MSWORLD.ORG

Wellness is a State of Mind

founded in 1996 MS World has grown from 6 people in a chat room to the largest all volunteer patients run organization worldwide, serving well over 225,000 members living with multiple sclerosis.

https://www.instagram.com/explore/tags/msworld1996/

Psychology Today Therapeutic Resource:
www.psychologytoday.com

Find a therapist in your area who can provide you with the help and support you need.

SUPPORTIVE LINKS:

- **facebook.com/nationalMSsociety**
- **walkMS.org**
- **youtube.com/nationalMSsociety**
- **challengewalk.org**
- **bikeMS.org**
- **twitter.com/MSsociety**
- **nationalMSsociety.org/navigator**
- **nationalMSsociety.org**
- **MSconnection.org/support**
- **nationalMssociety.org/supportgroup**

REFERENCES

All of the scriptural quotations and references have been taken from various versions of the Holy Bible, including: the King James Version, the New King James Version, the New International Version, the Easy English Bible, The Message Bible, the English Standard Version, the Amplified Bible, and the Holy Bible: Easy-to-Read Version, unless otherwise specified. Other translations include the English Revised Version, the International Standard Version, the New Living Translation, the Good New Translation (US Version), and the New American Standard Bible.

Askari, F., Ghajarzadeh, M., Mohammadifar, M., Azimi, A., Sahraian, M.A., & Owji, M. (2014). Anxiety in patients with multiple sclerosis: association with disability, depression, disease type and sex. Acta medica Iranica, 52 12, 889-92 .

Bhargava, P. (2015). Diet and Multiple Sclerosis. National Multiple Sclerosis Society.

Crayton, H. J., & Rossman, H. S. (2006). Managing the symptoms of multiple sclerosis: a multimodal approach. Clinical therapeutics, 28(4), 445-460.

Garfield, A. C., & Lincoln, N. B. (2012). Factors affecting anxiety in multiple sclerosis. Disability and rehabilitation, 34(24), 2047-2052.

National Multiple Sclerosis Society. (1997). Multiple Sclerosis Quality of Life Inventory: A User's Manual.

Provance, P. C. (2014). Physical therapy in multiple sclerosis rehabilitation. A Clinical Bulletin from the Professional Resource Center of the National Multiple Sclerosis Society.

Rudick, R. A., Cohen, J. A., Weinstock-Guttman, B., Kinkel, R. P., & Ransohoff, R. M. (1997). Management of multiple sclerosis. New England Journal of Medicine, 337(22), 1604-1611.

STAY FOCUSED, KEEP PRAYING
AND KEEP IT MOVING!!!!

CPSIA information can be obtained
at www.ICGtesting.com
Printed in the USA
JSHW071944281122
33973JS00004B/16